Help, it's My
...bly!

...urneys
...yone

First Published 2005
Whurr Publishers Ltd
The Atrium, Southern Gate,
Chichester, West Sussex PO19 8SQ
Telephone: (+44) 1243 779777
E-mail: cs-books@wiley.co.uk
Visit our home page on www.wiley.co.uk

British Library Cataloguing in Publication Data

A catalogue record for this book is available from the
British Library.

ISBN 1 86156 459 7

Printed and bound in the UK by TJ International Ltd,
Padstow, Cornwall.

Help, it's My Assembly!

Spiritual Journeys for Everyone

Hilary Broomfield and Brenda Webb

W
WHURR PUBLISHERS
LONDON AND PHILADELPHIA

'If there's no meaning in it,' said the King,
'that saves a world of trouble, you know,
as we needn't try to find any.'

Lewis Carol, *Alice in Wonderland*

Contents

Preface – Help, it's my assembly!

How do you feel when your name appears on the assembly rota? Or worse still when you are dropped on at the last minute to produce an assembly out of thin air? Is it something you relish or something you dread?

What goes through your mind? It has to be better than the last one? It has to be a bible story? It must entertain? It has to be deep and meaningful? Do you worry that some children can't join in? Or do you just want to get it over with? Let's be honest, we've all been there.

In the rush to get everything done, have you ever stopped and thought about why we have assemblies? Do we just do them because the government says so, or because we feel they are an opportunity for children to explore the who, what, where, and why of life, in other words their spirituality? Use the question boxes in part one to think about this some more.

If, like us, you feel assemblies should offer something significant, but doubt your ability to provide this or are concerned that your own faith or lack of it will get in the way, read on. Exploration of these very issues led to the writing of this book. If you are busy and short of time, read on, experience has led to a wealth of ideas which we hope will inspire and encourage you on your journey.

Part one

1. What does spirituality mean?

Try thinking of an acorn with spirituality as the 'essence' that causes it to become an oak.

In this way we can see our own spirituality as the essence of what it is to be human. Some have described it as the 'being' of a human being. Others might call it the spirit or the soul.

It is something we all feel and experience.

It is at the heart of ...

    feelings

        emotions

            and relationships.

It is at the root of...

    love

        empathy

            and compassion.

Through these we come to understand ourselves and others, identify and engage with our communities and gain insight into our world.

Our spirituality supports the growth of...

...now what would happen if...?

imagination,

creativity,

music,

art,

and

fun

and drives our quest for skills and learning.

For all, secular or religious, it is a fascinating journey, as it is through our spirituality that we can come to know who we are.

faith

Although the journey is personal, many experiences are common; in the everyday when we share a joke or kindness; in the special when we marvel at a DNA helix or gaze at the stars and wonder at the vastness of the universe and infinity.

belief

values

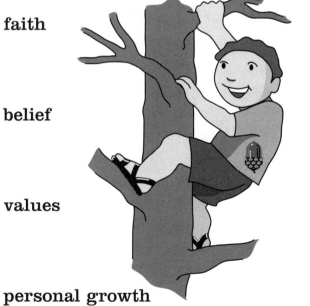

personal growth

Whoever we are our spirituality is there to be experienced and explored. There are different ways to travel and different paths to follow and each journey will be unique.

2. What part do school assemblies play?

On their spiritual journey, pupils need situations to challenge them to think, ask questions, and inspire their values and beliefs. These influence the way they choose to live their lives and guide their response to experiences along the way.

School assemblies can act as signposts, with the teacher as the encourager on the journey rather than the expert.

3. How can we encourage spiritual growth?

Just as an acorn needs warmth and nourishment to enable it to grow; spirituality also needs nurturing for its development. Throughout the first part of this book, we have used the symbol of the acorn to indicate helpful strategies. Your school assemblies can encourage spiritual growth by…

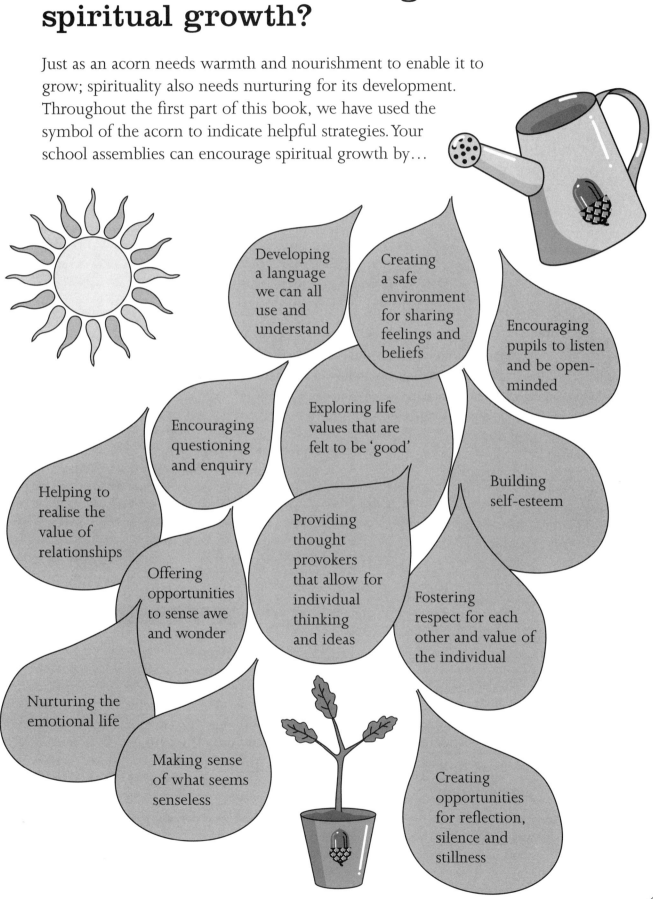

Developing a language we can all use and understand

Creating a safe environment for sharing feelings and beliefs

Encouraging pupils to listen and be open-minded

Encouraging questioning and enquiry

Exploring life values that are felt to be 'good'

Building self-esteem

Helping to realise the value of relationships

Providing thought provokers that allow for individual thinking and ideas

Offering opportunities to sense awe and wonder

Fostering respect for each other and value of the individual

Nurturing the emotional life

Making sense of what seems senseless

Creating opportunities for reflection, silence and stillness

Including everyone

Every school has a rich and diverse population of pupils, parents and staff. School assemblies are an ideal forum to bring all of these people together and build a sense of community, yet still recognise, respect and respond to difference. Inclusion means more than just 'being there' in a 'dump and hope' model (Corbett, 2002). It means everyone taking part in a way that is meaningful for them, whatever their background or ability or wherever they are on their personal journey. Trying to bring this about is a significant challenge, but the benefits for all are huge. So where do we begin?

BY LIFTING BARRIERS

You know when things have gone well. There is nothing like it! There is this amazing connection between yourself and the pupils. You can almost feel the thinking and learning taking place. And yet sometimes, something stops this from happening and gets in the way. These 'barriers to learning,' as described in the *Index for Inclusion*, (Booth et al, 2000) arise for different reasons. The challenge for us as assembly providers is to consider how we identify such barriers and try to lift them to make our assemblies more inclusive.

The *Index for Inclusion* poses some useful questions to help you make a start.

- ○ **Who is experiencing barriers to learning and participation?**

- ○ **What are these barriers?**

- ○ **How can they be minimised?**

- ○ **What resources are available to support this?**

Recognising barriers

Look closely at your assembly audience and think honestly about them. Are there some pupils who for one reason or another are not fully involved? Does everyone see, hear and understand what you are saying? Are they all able to take part in their own way and say what they think and feel? Or are some of them there, just in body but not in mind and spirit? Are some just sitting through, or having to leave halfway through, or maybe not coming in at all?

Barriers to learning do not arise exclusively from within individual pupils, and should not be seen as their 'fault'. They arise from the interaction between themselves and

- ◯ **their individual circumstances,**
- ◯ **the assembly leader,**
- ◯ **the assembly experiences offered,**
- ◯ **the community and environment in which the assembly takes place.**

For example, Katie, a Year One pupil enjoyed assemblies and always put her hand up to join in, despite having a significant hearing loss. No barriers to learning there. When she moved into Year Two, Katie's new teacher arranged for her to keep sitting near the front so she could still be close enough to hear. Katie continued to enjoy assemblies. But as Katie moved further up the school, her teachers said that she should sit with her own year group towards the back of the hall. After all she didn't want to sit with the little ones did she? Needless to say, Katie's involvement diminished along with her ability to hear and lip read what was going on. She wasn't one for causing trouble, and she didn't want to get teased about sitting with the 'babies', so she learned to switch off and dream about the weekend instead.

○ Where did the barrier to Katie's inclusion come from?

○ Can you identify pupils in your school who may be experiencing barriers to learning and participation in assemblies too?

Some will be more obvious than others, but remember, like Katie, not everyone makes a fuss! Children are no different from the rest of us; their own particular talents, difficulties, history and personality will affect them in a variety ways, as will the attitudes and teaching styles of individual teachers, along with whole school routines, policies and culture.

4. Understanding the barriers

The barriers to learning and participation will differ within each school. To help your thinking, we have used the three areas below, but recognise that there is a strong interface between all three.

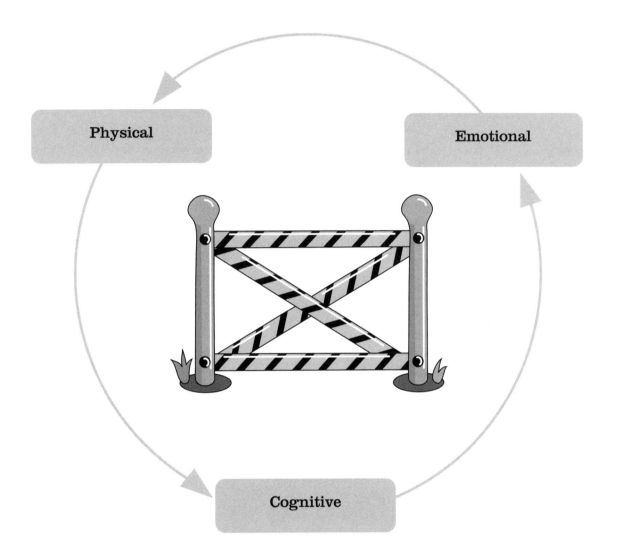

Read on to see how these clearly relate to current learning theory.

Physical barriers

discomfort

resources

impairment

distraction

illness

poor visibility or acoustics

access

○ Are these barriers to learning in your school?

○ What could you do about them?

Emotional barriers

low self-esteem

daily events

self consciousnesss

life story/personal history

motivation

poor social understanding of self and others

culture/ faith/beliefs

confusion

attitudes and values

isolation

behaviour

prejudice

fear

○ Are these barriers for any of your pupils?

○ What could you do to help?

Cognitive barriers

memory

attention span

learning ability

teaching style

learning style

complex ideas

language and communication

○ Do these create barriers for any of your pupils?

○ What could you do to help?

Overcome these barriers

 ## Overcome these barriers by . . .

O **providing** a comfortable, accessible and safe learning environment.

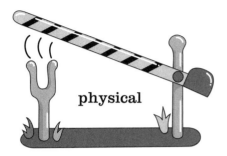

O **creating** an atmosphere of trust and respect where feelings, beliefs and values can be shared and explored.

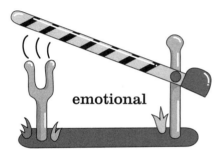

O **valuing and responding** to pupils' individual learning styles and support needs.

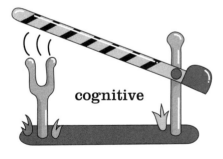

O **How does this inclusive practice connect with spiritual growth?**
Look back to page 5.

Now let's look at some of the ideas in more detail.

5. Unpacking the brain box

Recent research suggests that the brain works in three separate areas to influence our physical, emotional and cognitive responses. These areas are the reptilian brain, the limbic system and the neo-cortex (Shaw and Hawes, 1998). Understanding the role of each can help make us aware of why pupils come up against barriers to learning and participation and what resources we can use to help lift them.

A. Physical first

ARE YOU SITTING COMFORTABLY...?

We all know from experience that if Ben's legs are going dead from sitting on them, or Ali's jumper is itching, or Kim has come to school without breakfast, they will not be actively listening or involved in what is going on in assembly. They will not find even the most brilliant assembly an exciting or enjoyable experience! But it's no good our getting annoyed or frustrated. They cannot help it; their reptilian brain has hijacked their whole brain activity. When we are physically uncomfortable this area of our brain overrides or shuts down the two other areas, preventing us from concentrating, thinking, remembering or involving ourselves in what is going on around us. Biologically, it becomes increasingly impossible for us to learn. If pupils are to get the most out of our assemblies, we need to prevent or at least minimise their physical discomforts.

Lifting physical barriers

 Keep the reptilian brain happy and your pupils alert by ....

- **creating** a safe, welcoming atmosphere.
  Be ready in advance so you are at the front as the
  pupils gather. Smile and make eye contact.

- **arranging** for classes to sit in a familiar area
  and for some pupils the same seat.

- **making sure** all pupils can sit comfortably
  and be relaxed, especially those with physical
  difficulties and those who might not like being
  hemmed in.

- **remembering** that for some pupils (for example, those with Autistic
  Spectrum disorders), auditory and visual distractions can be physically
  uncomfortable.

- **checking** that all pupils can see what is going on, especially the visual
  aids, and that they can all hear clearly. If a disruption occurs, stop and
  refocus.

- **establishing** recognizable routines with a clearly defined beginning
  and end.

- **What are the physical distractions in your school that create barriers in assembly?**

- **What can you do about them?**

B. Emotional ease

Just being physically comfy in assembly isn't enough, we also have to feel emotionally safe and secure too. Look back at the oak tree on page 2 to see how personal feelings and spiritual growth are inextricably linked.

HOW ARE YOU FEELING?

Think of a memorable event. What you remember is probably what you 'felt' then. Emotions are a powerful prompt to memory. Think of a child in a war zone, the atrocities they have witnessed, etched indelibly on their mind through what they have seen, heard, touched and smelled. The memories, accompanied by related emotions such as fear, hatred, loneliness or despair, will continue to influence if, how and what they go on to learn. This is because the limbic system of our brain, which governs and uses our emotions, is also the area where our attitudes and values, our faith and beliefs, in other words our sense of identity and self-esteem, are rooted. It's the same for Lin who is anxious because of a situation at home; or Tim who is teased because of his faith; or Sabina who is sad because her rabbit has died. They 'can't think straight'. Their emotional state has become a barrier and assembly will pass them by. 'Continual emotional distress can create deficits in a child's intellectual abilities, crippling the capacity to learn' (Goleman, 1996).

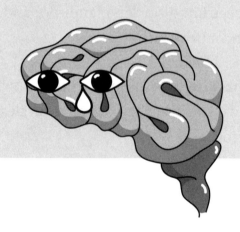

A driving force

See what happens when identity and emotion become interrelated:

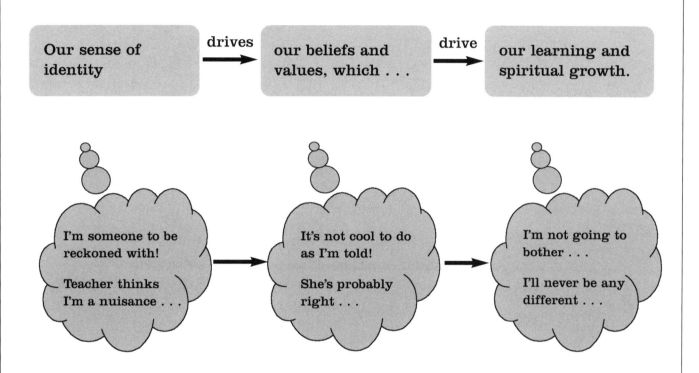

FEELING YOUR WAY

David Goleman (1996), a leading thinker in the area of 'emotional intelligence', believes that the link between our emotions and our learning is so important that he considers 'EQ' (emotional quotient) as equally important as 'IQ'. A high EQ leads to a well-balanced personality, with good 'intra' and 'inter' personal skills, and the ability to deal with the ups and downs of life. In this way it is not so much what you are born with, it is how you use what you have.

Lifting emotional barriers

 Keep the limbic brain happy and your pupils motivated by ....

○ **creating** situations in assembly where they feel good about themselves and can begin to confidently explore these attitudes.

○ **including** all pupils, even the ones who might not 'do it right'. Assembly is not a performance, rather a time to explore together. Include pupils who are 'in trouble', trying to relate to the person not their behaviour.

○ **making** assembly an enjoyable experience. Use a light touch involving positive emotions; humour, the ridiculous, joy, drama or suspense. They will make it memorable too. Negative emotions are infectious so enjoy your assembly!

○ **remembering** that everyone needs to feel comfortable about themselves, that they are included in what is taking place and that the assembly is relevant to them. The limbic system will then use it to build on and adapt current understanding of past experiences.

○ **being** generous with praise, even if the response isn't exactly what you were wanting! Make sure everyone feels encouraged.

○ **asking** staff to let you know of any pupils with a current 'worry'. They can then be sensitively and appropriately included.

○ **giving** yourself a pat on the back!

Responding to diversity

 Respond to the rich diversity of pupils in your school by ....

○ **opening up** assembly themes, prayers and reflections for everyone to share, whilst allowing for individual response.

○ **finding common ground** between different ethnic, cultural and faith perspectives, whilst respecting their distinctiveness.

○ **using multicultural sources**, artifacts and picture images to illustrate these.

○ **recognizing, respecting and responding** to physical, sensory and learning difference rather than disability and 'handicap'.

○ **promoting positive imagery** that avoids stereotyping.

○ **demonstrating** tolerance, understanding, and mutual respect and showing how damaging prejudice can be.

○ **involving** parents, religious and community leaders that reflect different groups within your locality.

○ **drawing from** the rich tapestry of stories and news events from across the world.

○ **celebrating** festivals from different religions.

○ **including** words, music and resources that use languages other than English.

○ **recognizing and celebrating** the achievements of all.

○ **What else could you be doing in your school?**

Mind-reading

Some pupils may have difficulty in understanding what feelings and emotions are, or be unable to express them. They may find it difficult to separate their own feelings from someone else's. The ability to reflect on events, personal feelings and the feelings of others is an essential part of school assembly and spirituality.

DO YOU KNOW HOW I FEEL?

The idea of individuals having a 'theory of mind' or 'mind-reading' (Howlin et al., 1999) has become topical in special education, particularly in the field of Autistic Spectrum Disorders (ASD). Interest in this has now widened to include those who do not have ASD, but nonetheless struggle with the 'emotional' and taking the perspective of other people. To understand what is meant by this, imagine buying a present for an elderly aunt. Are you able to put yourself in her shoes and buy the new Daniel O'Donnell CD for her cherished collection or will you buy Muddy Waters because you like the 'Blues'? But having a 'theory of mind' does not stop with such everyday matters; it goes much further. It is about the spiritual and the metaphysical, too. It leads us to recognise and value an 'inner life' bringing with it a 'reflective awareness' that nurtures spiritual growth, a sense of fulfilment and personal beliefs. It helps us recognise and understand that although other people's spiritual journeys may be different to our own, they are worthy of tolerance and respect. In this way, we would suggest that spiritual intelligence or 'SQ' is as essential as IQ and EQ.

Try to develop mind-reading

 Try to develop 'mind-reading' by giving opportunities to ....

○ **understand and talk** about feelings.

○ **realise** that although it can be difficult, feelings can be controlled.

○ **recognise** that other people have feelings too and that these may be different from our own.

○ **understand** that feelings affect behaviour.

○ **move** towards empathy, respect and compassion.

○ **respond and take action** on behalf of others.

Yummy! Mummy will be pleased that I like her birthday chocolates!

Techniques that help to include everyone

 Techniques that help to include everyone are...

○ **the use** of large photographs, cartoons of facial expressions or picture symbols representing emotions to illustrate how people are feeling, e.g. Jesus felt very angry.

○ **talking directly** about emotions and describing how they make us feel, e.g. *'When Jesus went into the temple he did not like what the people were doing. He felt very hot and his face was all red. His heart beat very fast. He shouted at all the people. He threw things around. He was so angry!'* In this way the pupils listening may be able to recall similar feelings that they might have experienced.

○ **using speech bubbles** to draw attention to people's words, e.g. Jesus said...

Make sure the bubble and text is large enough for everyone to see. These can be cards that are held up, or overhead transparencies. If the bubbles are made of large pieces of laminated card, and dry wipe pens are used, the bubbles can be reused and do not have to be made for each assembly.

○ **using thought bubbles** in the same way to show that people have information and thinking in their heads, e.g. Jesus thought…

○ **point out** how the thought and speech bubbles link together and relate them to the feelings described.

○ **use a 'swingometer'** or a sliding scale with a moving arrow to show the different feelings that someone might have during the course of a story or event. This can be marked in different ways to represent feelings or grades of feeling, e.g. an angry scale might have

Words – very calm, calm, a little bit angry, angry, very angry, etc

Colour – white for calm, with shades of pink, then red for anger

Numbers – scale of 1–10 (1 = calm, 10 = very angry)

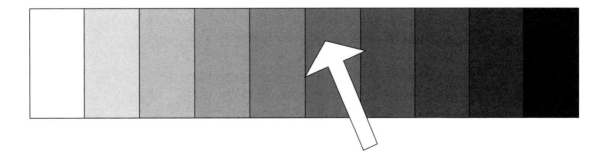

A happy scale using yellow and orange or a sad scale with shades of blue can be used in the same way.

○ if these devices are used as a regular event in assemblies, pupils will become familiar with the feelings and ideas they represent. If they are used to indicate what a child can directly see, such as a story being acted out, then they are much easier to interpret. Once they are understood, they can be used to refer back to past events that are no longer visible.

○ **relate** the feelings discussed in an assembly to everyday events in pupils' own lives where they might have felt similar emotions. It can be helpful for them to know that other people have the same feelings as themselves.

○ but **remember** to tread carefully, as this can have the potential for leaving some of those listening feeling vulnerable. We can never be sure what pupils or indeed colleagues have experienced and how deeply they feel about their past history. The recall of significant events can be powerful. Accept contributions to discussions that are volunteered, never force a response.

○ **How can you encourage 'mind-reading' in your assemblies?**

C. Thinking third

Does it make sense?

The final and by far the largest section of our brain pulls it all together. The neo-cortex sorts and orders all the information that bombards our brains.

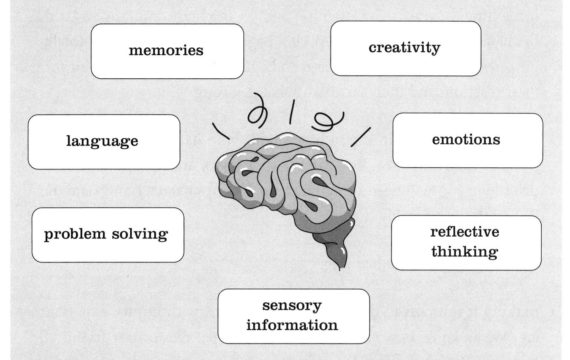

memories

creativity

language

emotions

problem solving

reflective thinking

sensory information

In making all these connections, it searches for patterns to help us make sense of our world. However, as assembly leaders, it is important and perhaps a relief to realise that we cannot impose a pattern on our pupils. Each one will have his or her own equally valid model of the world.

This is because we all have discrete ways of learning; preferred senses; particular abilities; varying concentration times and diverse experiences to build on.

Lifting cognitive barriers

 Keep the neo-cortex happy and your pupils involved in assembly by ....

○ **surprising** them! Use unusual or unexpected visual/audio aids, something to 'grab' their attention and set the brain thinking, e.g. dress in character (see assembly on p 103 'Bag lady'), hum or sing a totally unseasonal song – *Away in a manger* to begin Harvest assembly. Wait for their reaction, and then ask them what is wrong.

○ **making links explicit**. If you have pupils who have difficulty making sense of such surprises, for example those with autistic spectrum disorders, you will need to name the article or character and state the link with the assembly theme.

○ **building on** previous learning.

○ **making it relevant** to them. Make connections with pupils' experiences, e.g. 'We all know how sad we feel when our pet dies or our friend goes away' or 'Who has felt sad? Can anyone tell us what made them sad?' Use material and themes that are relevant to their lives.

○ **breaking** the assembly into short sections, e.g. repetitive patterns (see assembly on p 48 'All Change') or use changing activities or break up 'talk' with questions and opportunities for comment.

○ **giving** opportunities for them to use all their senses.

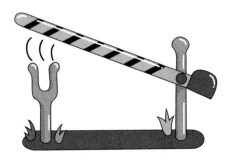

Connect with other learning

 Connect with other learning through ...

○ **making explicit links** with the assembly themes in other areas of the curriculum through cross-curricular work and a common 'vocabulary'. For example, the theme of 'sharing' can be explored in maths, through division or fractions; in drama, by pooling ideas, sharing space in PE, earth's resources in geography, the loaves and fishes in RE or looking up 'sharing' in a thesaurus during English.

○ **encouraging**....

... links made between all of life's experiences.

... an awareness of pattern and order in the world.

... quiet reflection.

... pupils to listen to each other and to God, if that is part of their understanding.

○ **enabling** pupils to reflect on assembly themes through "Branching Out" ideas (included in the assemblies in Part two) and any others they might suggest.

○ **following up** their thoughts, where possible, using a multi-sensory approach; through drawing, sculpting and modelling, composing music, mime or storytelling.

○ **recognising and valuing** the sometimes inexplicable 'otherness' that is part of some pupils' experience and individual faith beliefs and experiences.

6. Supporting different learning styles

Our senses are important to the neo-cortex. Vast amounts of information are fed to our brains through our senses and although all of them play a part, research has shown that most individuals will learn more efficiently through one in particular. Just as different plants have preferred care needs to flourish,

so individual pupils have preferred learning needs to flourish. Visual learners (V) tend to prefer the use of pictures and the written word; auditory learners (A), the spoken word and sound effects; kinaesthetic learners(K), hands on practical tasks, drama and role play.

Using a combination of these will create a multi-sensory approach which benefits all learners. Trevor Hawes (Shaw and Hawes, 1998) refers to it as 'VAKing' a lesson. This will help remove the barriers to learning and participation that are created from adopting just one teaching style, and will provide alternative means of expression for those who have difficulty accessing or using spoken language.

To offer our pupils the best opportunity to be challenged, ask questions or be inspired and for our assemblies to act as the signposts we mentioned earlier, we need to ask...

○ **How can we include something for everyone in our assemblies?**

Keep the visual learner involved

 Keep the visual learner involved through...

written words

I see what you mean!

real objects and artifacts

pictures and cartoons

TV and video clips

symbols and rebuses

flipcharts

OHP transparencies

○ Pupils, who prefer this way of learning, may also include those with impaired hearing and pupils with Down's syndrome. See 'Every picture tells a story' (Empathy p 74)

Keep the auditory learner involved

 Keep the auditory learner involved through...

spoken words
and storytelling

I hear what
you're saying

discussion

voice effects,
through change
in pitch, volume,
accent

rhythmic words
and refrains

repetitive phrases

sound effects

song

musical
instruments
and percussion

mood music

○ Pupils, who prefer this
way of learning, may
also include those with
impaired sight and
pupils with William's
syndrome. See 'Prayers
and Thinking' in 'A sad
state of affairs' (Sadness
and loss p 62)

Keep the kinaesthetic learner involved

 Keep the kinaesthetic learner involved through...

sign language

symbolic gesture, such as a clenched fist to represent anger

Can I have a go?

physical actions and movements to carry out

practical tasks such as cut and paste

mime

acting out stories and events

making sound effects

moving and positioning props

pointing

change of posture

drawing and writing on flip charts/in the air

○ Pupils, who prefer this way of learning, may also include those with impaired sight and those who have difficulty with attention and sitting still! See 'The thirsty crow' (Patience p 61)

7. Getting the message across

Our words can be spoken, signed or symbolised; but first and foremost they are about ideas. Effective communication is about meaning.
Is the person speaking able to say what they mean and is the person listening able to understand what is said? Are the ideas behind the words clear? Do the speaker and listener connect?
Or is something preventing the message from getting through? What form of support do we need to put in place in our assemblies to make sure the line is clear?

DO YOU UNDERSTAND?

Our understanding of words is greatly affected by the context in which we hear them. Think of Sally, aged 14 months, who seems to understand every word of 'What a glorious day, I think we'll go for a walk in the park and feed those greedy ducks!' Or does she? The exact meaning of the word 'glorious' is probably beyond her, but she does understand where she is going, what she is going to do and that it's a fun thing to do. That's because the words were spoken by Mummy, as she got out the push chair and Sally's coat, and then Mummy smiled as she put bread in her pocket. The extra 'clues' that helped Sally understand are often referred to as 'scaffolding'. In time, her understanding will grow, as she hears the words again in different contexts and begins to try them out for herself. And so, in the same way as a builder uses the support of scaffolding around a house, to reach greater heights than he would do without it, Sally is able to understand the complex language and ideas she hears through the additional support her mother gives her.

... so what you're saying is ...

Support understanding

 Support understanding through...

○ **deciding on the key ideas** you want the pupils to think about.

○ **using key words or phrases** to reflect those ideas and help understanding.

○ **repeating these key words** frequently during the assembly.

○ **using repeating refrains** for the pupils to join in.

○ **adjusting the complexity** and length of sentences you use. Short sentences are easily understood. Children remember them. They can still carry important ideas.

○ **using dual language** presentation if appropriate.

○ **preparing pupils in advance** for key vocabulary before the assembly begins.

○ **using extra VAK clues** to meaning (see p 28).

○ **using facial expression**, gesture and body language to support your words.

○ **using speech and thought bubbles** (see pp 22–23) to keep the ideas behind spoken language visible.

○ **signing** using Makaton, BSL or rebuses (see p 61).

○ **using attention grabbers** such as story boxes, mystery envelopes, lucky bags, puppets, suitcases, hats, musical effects, telescopes, reporter's microphone, etc.

○ **involving pupils in touching** artifacts, writing on flip charts, sequencing pictures, voting with a show of hands.

○ **involving the audience as a whole** through becoming a waving crowd, the roar of a lion, the ticking of a clock, the rocking movement of a train.

Give everyone a voice

 Give everyone a voice through...

○ **ensuring** that everyone has a chance to answer and the more vocal and confident pupils do not dominate.

○ **encouraging** less verbal pupils to reply, by a show of hands, an individual word, a finger point, holding a picture symbol, a nod of the head.

○ **offering** structured choices, e.g. 'Do you think Daniel felt sad or frightened?'

○ **drawing** pupil responses, back into the assembly, so that everyone has heard and appreciates the contribution, e.g. 'I agree with Lucy, I think Daniel must have felt frightened when he saw the lion's teeth. What do the rest of you think?'

○ **considering** the type and complexity of the questions you ask. Your choice will depend on who you are speaking to and the sort of answers you are seeking.

○ **using** 'When', 'What', 'Where', 'Which' or 'Who' will elicit straightforward factual replies.

○ **asking** 'Do you'...or 'Is'... or 'Did' will give a yes/no answer.

○ **beginning with** 'How' or 'Why' makes the question more open-ended and is more searching.

○ **dealing** tactfully with unexpected or seemingly unrelated answers, without making the child feel put down. Can you use what they have said in some way? If not, there is a real skill in thanking every contribution no matter how off beam it might seem!

○ **What extra communication support could you include?**

8. Time to travel

So the next time it is your assembly...

take with you...

an understanding
of spirituality,

information on
how the brain
works,

knowledge of
barriers
to learning,

insights into
different learning
styles,

confidence in
what to do . . .

. . . and how to
do it.

Then choose a theme from Part two and you're ready to go!

Part two

1. How to use Part two

Themes

Choose one of the 40 different themes. We have organised them into four aspects of spirituality. These are:

- **Ourselves** – explores personal feelings and reactions to life events.

- **Others** – covers building relationships and understanding other people.

- **Community** – encourages identifying and engaging with community groups and understanding the rights and responsibilities of citizenship.

- **World** – fosters an insight into global issues and inspires a sense of awe and wonder.

Instant and prepared

Each theme has two formats.

 Instant assemblies – can be picked up and used without any preparation. We assume you will have a flip chart, marker pens, scissors and Blu tac.

 Prepared assemblies – use visual aids, props and ideas that need preparation in advance.

All the assemblies are 'VAKed' and designed to appeal to different learning styles. They can be run by an assembly leader, groups of pupils or whole classes. A few need the help of colleagues.

66 Quote for the day

These are for you. They are included to open up your thinking.

Prayers and thinking

Some people find this part of assembly 'difficult'. We have tried to design the prayers and reflections so that everyone can feel comfortable and included. They provide moments for

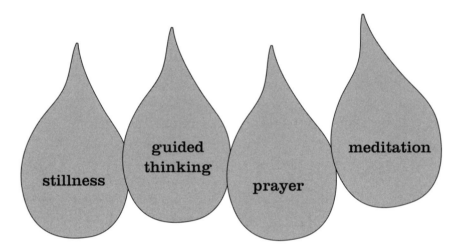

Try signalling the beginning of this time with the lighting of a candle or the ringing of an Indian bell. Use the same sound and the blowing out of the candle to signal when it is over. As you light the candle you could say 'Time for prayers and thinking.'

Faith links

Each assembly has a Christian link and a further one with another world religion.

The use of music

Music is important. It can create mood, quieten pupils, be linked to a theme or reflection. Songs and hymns should reflect the theme of the assembly.

Branching out

These are for you and the pupils . . .

To ask
questions

To widen
appreciation of
an assembly
theme

To link with
other learning

To explore
values and beliefs
in small groups

As a starting
point for further
assemblies

To practise
using some of the
key vocabulary

To hear what
other people
think

2. Assemblies

Ourselves

Temper, temper!

The final straw

YOU WILL NEED

A flip chart, pen, coloured straws (or cut thin strips of coloured paper as you talk), scissors and Blu-Tack.

(Draw a camel with gnashing teeth and a speech bubble with 'Grrr' inside.)

Have you ever heard of the saying 'the straw that broke the camel's back'? Well this is Cedric and I'm going to show you what this means. Cedric is grumpy. He's always letting little things get on top of him and make him cross. For instance, he forgot to put his alarm on last night, so he got up late. Let's put this straw on here to help us remember that. (**Stick a straw on his back.**) Because he was late, he had to rush. (**Call out a pupil to stick a straw above the other one as if building a pile.**) Cedric had no time for breakfast so he left the house feeling hungry. (**Add a straw.**) Because he set off late, he got stuck in a camel jam. (**Add a straw.**) Cedric tried to take a short cut, but there were desert works and he had to wait. (**Add a straw.**) When he got to work late his boss told him off. (**Add a straw.**) Not only did he tell him off, he did it in front of the other camels. (**Add a straw.**) Cedric thought they were all laughing at him. (**Add a straw.**) The load he carried felt heavier than usual because of all the extra straws and grumpiness he was carrying. (**Add a straw.**) When his best friend asked if he was alright he thought she was teasing him. It was the final straw. (**Add a straw.**) and he flew into a rage, kicking sand in her eyes. His poor friend didn't know what she had done! We can all be like Cedric sometimes, collecting problems like straws. We let little things build up until we snap. We need to try and see them as the little things they are and like straws let them blow away in the wind. (**Let some straws drop from your hand.**)

Prayers and Thinking

Close your eyes and think of a special place that makes you feel calm and safe and quiet. It might be a real place or a place you make up in your head. As you think of that place listen to these words, relax, and breathe deeply from your stomach.

Help us to learn how to control our anger. Teach us to look at problems in a calm way and to ask for help when we need it. *Amen.*

Next time you feel angry try this again.

Quote for the day

Forgo your anger for a moment and save yourself a hundred days of trouble.
Chinese Proverb

Faith links

Christian
Jesus's anger in the temple Luke 19, 45–48

Buddhist
How violence is ended in the story of Brahmadatta and Digniti

Branching out

 Make some calming traffic lights Red means stop. Amber means take time to think. Green means go and talk to someone or sort out the problem calmly.

 As a group, think of some little things that make you angry. Make the word 'angry' out of straws as you do this and then blow the word away.

 Produce a set of illustrated step by step recipe cards or pages in a cook book for making a 'chilled out cookie'.

A recipe for success

PREPARATION NEEDED

A chef's hat and apron

A saucepan

A recipe book

An imitation hob (e.g. an upturned cardboard box with a ring on)

A dishcloth

A picture symbol or photo representing anger

A flip chart and pen

I like cooking. **(Put on your chef's hat and apron.)** To be a good cook it's important to have the right ingredients **(hold up a bottle of milk)**, the right tools **(hold up a saucepan)** and the right recipe **(flick through a cook book)**. But no matter how good a cook you are sometimes things still go wrong. Take heating up milk for example. Even though I've got the milk and the right tools and I know what to do **(pour some milk in a saucepan and pretend to put it on a hob)**, it still sometimes turns out wrong. I forget what I'm meant to do **(walk off and leave it, reading the cookery book)**. I let the milk get out of control and it boils over **(rush back to the pan and switch off the hob)**. It makes a terrible mess, frothing up and splashing and spitting everywhere, burning on the cooker. It takes ages to sort it out afterwards **(mop up the mess with a cloth)**. It really makes me angry when it happens. I blame the milk; I blame the saucepan and the cooker **(bang things about)** and anyone else that's around. If only they had all worked properly, things wouldn't have got out of control and I wouldn't have had this problem. **(Shout out and shake your finger at the audience.)** It's all your fault! **(Throw your hat and apron on the floor and stomp off.)**

(Come back and pick up the things and start to tidy up.) Of course afterwards I feel really stupid. Fancy getting cross about a bit of spilt milk! I suppose I shouldn't really have walked off and left the milk in the first place. Perhaps all this wouldn't have happened then. Now I feel bad about losing my temper. I feel really silly for shouting like that. I hope I didn't hurt anyone? **(Ask the audience.)** You see feeling angry **(hold up symbol)** is a bit like a pan of milk boiling over. The anger feels hot and bubbly inside of us. And if we don't learn how to turn it down, it can bubble right up and get out of control. Anger can splash out all over the place, just like the milk. If it's really bad, it can hurt other people, just like the hot milk could.

It's not wrong to feel angry. Everyone does sometimes; it's a thing that we all feel. I expect some of you have. What sorts of things have happened to you to make you feel that way? **(Listen to a few examples.)** We often feel cross when things don't work out the way we wanted them to **(Refer back to the examples just given.)** We feel cross with ourselves and other people too. But getting into a rage and shouting and throwing things, or hitting out at other people isn't the way to sort it out. When we get really angry, we often end up hurting the ones we love the most, our family and friends. We usually end up hurting ourselves too because we feel bad inside, or because the people we hurt don't want to be with us any more.

The important thing is trying to control that anger and not let it boil over like the milk. What sorts of things are helpful to you when you want to keep calm? **(Write these up on a flip chart.)** What we have here in these ideas is the beginning of a really good recipe just like those in my cook book. Only this is a recipe for understanding and dealing with anger. It's a recipe for a chilled out cookie. **(Draw a biscuit shape with a smiley face on it.)** Try to take some time to sort out a recipe that works for you, it's worth it, and then you can be a chilled out cookie too!

Alpha to omega

From kick-off to final whistle

(Read the words.) Ask what letter is at the beginning of the alphabet. **(Pupil to write on flip chart.)** Ask what letter is at the end of the alphabet. **(Pupil write on flip chart.)** Ask what letter is at the beginning and end of BED. **(Write them up.) (Try other words.)**

This is a story about Ali who didn't begin or end. Ali joined the local junior football team. He had always dreamed of being a champion footballer and went to every training session. **(Get 'Ali' out to mime dribbling, heading etc.)** This week he had been chosen as Sub. He ran out proudly in his red and green strip. 'I'll score the best goal ever', he told the coach. **(Assembly cheer – 'come on Ali'.)**

The game kicked off. **(Write under BEGINNING.)** Ali sat on the bench watching. **(Sit Ali on a chair.)** If only he could get on the pitch, he would score not one goal, but three goals. Just after half-time Ali was sent on. **(Cheer Ali as he runs up and down.)** Jez passed the ball to John. John turned to pass it to Ali but Ali went the other way. The other team got the ball and scored. 'What are you doing?' yelled the coach 'Watch the ball'. Poor Ali didn't know what to do. He was terrified, what if he tried but missed the goal. Everyone would laugh at him. He'd look busy, but keep away from the ball. And that was what he did for the rest of the game until the final whistle. **(Write under END.)** The score stayed at 1–0.

Ali had the chance to begin by getting the ball and end by scoring a goal. Why didn't he? The coach had a word with Ali and helped him not to be frightened. The next match he scored three goals!

Sometimes we don't start or finish things because we are afraid or we can't be bothered. **(List things we don't BEGIN. List things we don't END. Ask why.)** Let's make up our minds to always have a go.

Prayers and Thinking

Have two pupils hold a length of string or a metre rule or stand at the beginning and end of a row

Say … 'Lots of prayers begin "Dear God" **(indicate the beginning of the string)** and end "Amen" **(end of the string)**. In the middle you can ask for help to begin something new. If you prefer not to pray you can think of standing at the beginning of the string, then think of something new you want to do in the middle and say 'I will do it' at the end. Think or pray as I walk from the beginning to the end of the string.

Faith links

Christian
Jesus's death and resurrection
Mark 15+16

Buddhist
Pirith, marking an ending

Branching out

 In groups, all begin with the same word and make a word chain. The second word beginning with the last letter of the first, etc. Read the chains. See how they all **began** the same but had different **ends.** Track how they got there.

 Listen to a different creation story.

 Write a birth announcement and an epitaph for a character from a book, historical figure, famous person.

Memories

PREPARATION NEEDED

Either 2 school bags:

1 filled with items that are brought to school;

1 with 7 large coloured 'think bubbles' labelled: I remember, angry, sad, happy, exciting, funny, scary (each with a relevant facial expression)

Or a group of pupils each with one item in their bag

Another group of pupils each with one think bubble in their bag

Picture of a happy face and a sad face

Flip chart divided down the centre, one side marked 'Beginning' the other side marked 'End'

Music – 'Memories' from CATS (optional)

(*suggestions for a leavers' assembly – pupils or staff)

(*Have the two bags on a table or groups lined up either side at the front.)* Ask who brings a bag to school. What do they put in it? What do they think is in the bags at the front? Suggest the owners show us what is inside. **(Pull out items from bag 1 or group 1, one at a time.)** Discuss with the pupils why they bring these things to school, e.g. lunch-box, pencil case, trainers, include a humorous item. **(Owner holds each item at 'Beginning' side of the flip chart.)** Point out these are the things we bring to school at the beginning of the day. Ask for suggestions of what they take home from school at the end of the day. (They will probably repeat some of the things from the bags and also include notes, homework, etc.)

Suggest there are other things they take home at the end of each day that are invisible. Ask if they have any idea what they might be. Suggest you might find them in the other bag(s). **(Take out the 'I remember' think bubble.)** Read it. Point out that at the end of each day, we take home memories we didn't have at the beginning of the day.

(*If a leavers' assembly, we leave with lots of memories we didn't have when we began.)

(Take out the 'think bubbles' one at a time.) Read them and ask who would like to share an example of each memory from yesterday, last week, last year, etc.

Reinforce what kind of memory it is by pointing to the face on the bubble. **(Have pupils hold the bubbles at 'End' side of the flip chart.)**

(*If leavers' assembly, ask staff to share an early memory of each pupil/group leaving, beginning 'I remember when…')

Ask if memories come at the beginning or end of something. **(Indicate the 'End' side of the flip chart.)**

Explain the end of today means there will be a new beginning tomorrow. Ask if anyone can think how our memories can help us with new beginnings, e.g. Mrs Brown did not like my mouse in her drawer! I have a funny memory **but** I will not bring my mouse to school again tomorrow! Tim was kind to me today that gave me a happy memory. I will make someone happy tomorrow. **(Put the relevant think bubble in the bag.)** Take it to the beginnings side saying I will remember not to… or I must remember to…..

Take a couple of minutes to think of a special memory.

(*Those leaving will be taking home a bag full of special memories, but they will take a new bag to their new school to fill up with new memories. Put an empty bag on the back of a leaver and get them to lead all leavers round the hall.)

Quote for the day
'Begin at the beginning,' the King said, gravely, 'and go on till you come to the end; then stop'. Lewis Carrol (1832–1898) *Alice in Wonderland*.

All change

All change

We are all going on a train journey with Ted from John O' Groats to Land's End. **(Practise pupils quietly chanting 'John O' Groats to Land's End' to a train rhythm (or tapping knees). Start and stop with a hand signal.(+))**

Ted is going to visit a friend. **(Sits in train.)** He has bought a ticket; found out the time of a train; which platform to get on; and packed his lunch. Ted is shy and gets a bit worried when others get on the train. **(Passengers get on.)** Off they go (+)… Ted doesn't know what to say to the others. Suddenly, one of them offers to put Ted's bag on the rack. **(Mime.)** Ted says thankyou and soon they are chatting.

When the train reaches GLASGOW it stops. Ted is surprised to hear the Guard call 'All change'. **(Everyone gets out.)** Ted is worried, he doesn't like changing trains. **(Mime.)** Another train comes and he gets on. **(Sits in 'new' train.)**

More new passengers get on. **(Fill seats.)** The train leaves. (+) Ted still feels shy. Suddenly he remembers and offers to put a lady's case on the rack. Soon they are chatting and Ted is feeling pleased with himself. When the train reaches CARLISLE it stops. 'All change,' calls the guard. 'Not again!', thinks Ted. **(All get off.)** Ted gets on the next train, he doesn't like changing trains. More passengers get on too **(fill seats)** and the train starts off. (+) Ted looks around 'That boy looks bored, I'll ask him to play "I-Spy".' **(Play and assembly join in)** They were having fun. Suddenly the train stops. 'All change,' calls the guard. 'I don't belive it!' moans Ted, as he gets off with the other passengers. 'But I'm beginning to get used to it.' 'Train for Land's End,' calls the guard. 'At last,' sighs Ted, getting on with the others. **(All get on.)** 'What shall I do on this train?' **(Ask for ideas of what Ted can do.)** When Ted got off at Land's End he was feeling very pleased with himself.

Ask when did Ted feel worried. **(Changes.)** What changes worry us? **(Draw two or three suitcases on top half of paper and write worries on them.)** Ted started on his journey very worried **(draw worried face)** but was much happier at the end. **(Draw happier face.)** Why was Ted happier?

Branching out

 Make a simple Origami model.

 Brainstorm changes in nature, e.g. caterpillar to butterfly, weather, acorn to oak.

 Write a poem beginning each verse 'I will build with bricks of … (e.g. truth, kindness, patience, love) a school/ home/world where …'

Grand designs

PREPARATION NEEDED

A building site set up at the front (e.g. sand, wheelbarrow, bricks, spade, boots, mugs, lunch box, etc)

3 hard hats one labelled FOREMAN)

table

bucket labeled HARD WORK CEMENT

trowel

trampette or deep crash mat

floral oasis blocks or soft bricks

labels for different curriculum areas to stick on the bricks

sign (**_name of school_ BUILDERS – BEST IN THE BUSINESS**)

(If transfer assembly, a 'Master Builder' certificate for each pupil transferring)

<u>Leader </u>walk round 'building site', singing *Bob the Builder*. Ask about some of the equipment. Explain they are going to think about all the building that has been going on in _____ School. Call out two pupils. Put on hard hats.

Give each a pile of oasis/soft 'bricks'. Have a race to build a tower, one standing on the trampette (this should wobble and fall), the other on a table. Discuss difficulties – wobbly ground is not a good place to build – building needs a firm foundation (like the table).

Explain school is like a building site. Read the school sign together. Sing '___ School Builders, can they fix it?' to *Bob the Builder* tune (or chant). Pupils reply 'Yes they can'.

Ask where/when they last saw building going on in school. Explain a special building is being constructed that will not fall down. Stick a label to a brick, e.g. *spelling*. Ask who's getting better at *spelling*, call out one pupil. Ask why or how they are getting better.(Hard work.)

Ask them to put on a hard hat. Cover their brick with a trowel of imaginary HARD WORK CEMENT and begin to build a wall on the table.
Repeat using the other labels, e.g. *PE handwriting, keyboard skills, IEP targets*. You

can sing the *Bob the Builder* song inserting each pupil's name.

(If this is a transfer assembly use subjects relevant to the pupils who are transferring and mention all their names. They stand at the front.)

Ask who checks that the work on a building site is done properly and built on a firm foundation.(Hold up FOREMAN hat.) Who helps you to understand it? (Teachers.)

Ask a teacher to come out and wear the foreman hat.

(If transfer assembly- teacher of transfer class comes to join the pupils.)

Sing '_____the FOREMAN can he/she fix it' pupils reply. 'Yes he/she can.'

Sum up _____School Builders are the best in the business. All we learn is made on a firm foundation so we can go on building walls of learning like the one on the table.

(If transfer assembly add... 'When you go to your new class/school what you have learned will not "fall down" because you have built on a firm foundation with lots of hard work.')

Hand out certificates.

You don't have to be big to be brave!

Scared Stanley

(Draw a stick man representing 'Scared Stanley Small' in the middle of a large sheet of paper.) Explain that Stanley is only three feet tall. He is the smallest boy in his school and down his street, and sometimes he gets scared of things. He wishes he was bigger and braver. Explain that we all feel like that sometimes. Talk about what Stanley feels like when he is scared, e.g. shaky, feeling sick, hot, wanting to run away. Describe a time when you felt scared just like Stanley, choosing something that others might not be scared of. Explain that not everyone is scared of the same thing. What do the children think Stanley could be scared of?

(Write up their ideas around his picture.)

Go back to how you faced up to the fear you spoke of earlier, and how you felt afterwards. Ask the children to come up with a helpful idea for each thing that scares Stanley. Try to include solutions that he can manage himself and those that involve others. Explain that being brave doesn't mean we have to face our fears alone, our friends, family and teachers can help us. We need to learn to believe in ourselves and that we can do difficult things.

(Write the helpful ideas next to the scary words. Each time you do this give Stanley a medal for believing that he can do something about his fears. Finally count up the medals and change his name to 'Brave Stanley Small'.) Explain that although he is still only three feet tall, it doesn't matter. You don't have to be big to be brave.

Prayers and Thinking

We all feel scared sometimes, no matter how big or small or young or old we are. Help us to be brave and believe we can do difficult things.

(Draw a big gold medal on a sheet of paper.)
This is a special medal for being brave about something that scares you. Try and see this medal around your neck as you think or pray about being brave.

Quote for the day

The brave man carves out his fortune, and every man is the sum of his works
Miguel De Cervantes (1547–1616) *Don Quixote*

Faith links

Christian and Jewish
David and Goliath
1 Samuel 17: 19-51

Branching out

 Make up a poem that starts 'Scared Stanley Small wasn't very tall.' Use a scary font when Stanley is scared. Use a bold font when he is being brave.

 Design and make some certificates and medals to present to people in the class for when they have been brave.

 In pairs, role play a news reporter interviewing Stanley or Little Green Caterpillar.

Sports day at the zoo

PREPARATION NEEDED

A set of pictures:
  a line of cones
  a balance beam
  a water splash
  a barrel
  a scramble net
  a finishing line

Competitor numbers
1–5 with the names
Zebra, Rhino, Lion,
Elephant, Caterpillar

Safety pins, a gold
medal and a
microphone

WHAT TO DO

The assembly presenter
acts as sports
commentator, holding
up the pictures to show
progress in the race. The
audience are the
cheering crowd and five
volunteers the animals.

(Commentator holds microphone.)
Good morning and welcome to Sports Day at the Zoo. My name is Mr/Mrs R.U. Ready, and I am your commentator for the obstacle race.

(Invite the audience to act as the crowd. Introduce each competitor pinning on their number. The competitors should act out what you say and the presenter should encourage the crowd to cheer each one.)

First of all we have **NUMBER ONE – ZEBRA**, running in black and white today. Zebra is extremely fast and can run like the wind. There's no crossing him! Next we have **NUMBER TWO – RHINO**. He gets his head down and just charges along! **NUMBER THREE** in the race is **LION**. A very aggressive competitor, listen to him roar! And look at him flex those muscles – he must be in with a strong chance! Running as **NUMBER FOUR** is **ELEPHANT**. There's no forgetting him! He never gets in a flap, despite those ears. He can lift anything with the power he packs in that trunk. And finally we have **NUMBER FIVE**… **LITTLE**….. **GREEN CATERPILLAR**. Ranked as an outsider, he doesn't carry the same weight as the others. Some have even said he is too small and is a bit of a joke. Still you never know. The plucky little chap is bravely going to give it a go.

(Describe the race, indicating progress through the pictures and sitting down each competitor as they are eliminated.)

The competitors take their place at the starting line, they are under starter's orders… and they're off! *(Crowd cheers.)* Oh dear… **ZEBRA** is in trouble already, he has run so fast, that he has run past all the obstacles without trying any and has been disqualified. *(Crowd boos.)* **RHINO** has made a good start with his head down, but has charged straight through the cones. He's all over the place and has been told to leave the course. *(Crowd boos.)* **LION** roars along as expected but has just stopped still at the water splash. He dips in a toe… he's shaking his head… the water is just too cold. He has dropped out of the race. *(Crowd boos.)* **ELEPHANT** keeps calm, no flapping here, he is making good progress but…oh …he's gone and got stuck inside the barrel, he's not going anywhere. *(Crowd boos.)* Now **LITTLE GREEN CATERPILLAR**, gets off to a very slow start, but is gradually catching up *(Crowd cheers.)*… In and out the cones… across the balance beam… through the water splash as fast as all those little legs will carry him… he squeezes past **ELEPHANT** who is still stuck in the barrel… inches his way up the scrambling net, and down the other side to the finishing line. Ladies and Gentleman …he has done it! **LITTLE GREEN CATERPILLAR** has won the race! *(Crowd cheers wildly.)*

(Present the medal and speak to the crowd.)

So, who would have believed it! Little Green Caterpillar might not have been as big as the rest but he has shown outstanding bravery against all the odds. It just shows what you can do if you believe in yourself and you keep on going! And remember…you don't have to be big to be brave!

Get me out of this!

All at sea

YOU WILL NEED

Flip chart and marker pens

TO DO

Arrange 8 chairs in a boat shape, seats facing inwards. Divide assembly into 2 groups to make sound effects which change as the storm gets rougher. Practise **WIND** and **WAVE** noises, gradually getting louder:
WIND: (a) gentle blowing × 3, (b) sshhh × 3, (c) howling and waving arms × 3.
WAVES: (a) slip-slop × 3, (b) slip-slop woosh × 3, (c) slip-slop, crash × 3.
Tell the story, encourage travellers to mime the story and encourage all pupils to copy your actions

Today you are going to help me tell a story from the Bible.

(Call out a pupil to be Paul.) Paul, a Christian, had been captured. He was being sent by boat to see the Emperor. *(Sit 'Paul' in the front seat.)* Other prisoners were going with him. *(Fill up other seats.)* They pulled up the sail and set off along the coast in a gentle breeze. *(Sway.)*

The **WIND** was blowing. *(Blowing.)* The **WAVES** rippled under the boat. *(Slip-slop.)* But it wasn't long before a strong **WIND** got up *(sshhh)* and the **WAVES** began to get rough. *(Slip-slop, woosh.)*

(Sway more vigorously.) The men began to feel afraid. *(Draw frightened face on flip chart.)* It was hard to stand up and they had to put ropes round the ship to keep it together. *(Repeat wind and waves.)*

The **WIND** got stronger. *(Howling and waving arms.)* The **WAVES** got rougher. *(Slip-slop, crash.)* The boat was rolling from side to side *(roll)*, the sails were ripping, the noise was deafening, *(hands over ears)* it was very dark. *(Hands over eyes.)* Paul and the men were terrified and feeling very sick. *(Repeat getting louder, add beads of sweat to face on flipchart.)* 'Get us out of this,' they yelled. They threw everything into the sea to make the ship lighter. Still the **WIND** howled and the **WAVES** crashed. Then Paul stood up 'Don't be frightened,' he shouted, 'last night, an angel told me that God will keep us safe and I believe God.' The **WIND** still howled. The **WAVES** still crashed. The men were still terrified, they thought they would crash *(loud clap)* on the rocks.

Many days later the boat ran aground and smashed. 'Swim for it,' shouted the men. They all jumped off and swam to the shore. *(Point to face and ask, why the men were afraid; why Paul stopped being afraid; what frightens us? Write ideas round face.)* Affirm everyone feels afraid sometimes but we can get through it like the men on the boat.

Prayers and Thinking

(Draw a scared face on the flip chart.)

We all have things that frighten us Can you make a frightened face? Change to a smile as you think of something you are no longer frightened of. You can say thank you to God for always being with you when you are afraid.

Quote for the day

Let me assert my firm belief that the only thing we have to fear is fear itself.
Franklin D Roosevelt (1933) First Inaugural Address

Faith links

Christian and Jewish
Elijah hiding from God, 1 Kings 19: 1–7

Christian
Jesus in the Garden of Gethsemene
Matthew 26: 36

Branching out

 Look at the Emergency Rescue symbols in the telephone directory. Design your own rescue symbols for when you are afraid.

 Listen to the story of The Three Little Pigs or other. Put up your hand when you think they feel frightened.

Make scary masks. Have a parade to decide which is the most scary.

Help, I need somebody

PREPARATION NEEDED

A sliding scale (see p. 23) graded: OK – frightened – very frightened – terrified

a cartoon face for each degree of fear

a big black, hairy spider

set of emergency rescue symbols (from phone book)

WHAT TO DO

Prepare 2–3 pupils to mime situations where they are afraid, showing varying degrees of fear, e.g. a spider in the bath, in the dentist, being sent to the head teacher.

Ask a colleague to yell, look afraid and call for help when you/leader drop a spider on their lap.

(Let the pupils realise you are up to something, perhaps be singing 'Little Miss Muffet'. Drop the spider into colleague's lap from behind. They yell and call for someone to remove it.)

Leader: What a lot of fuss! It was only a toy spider. **(To pupils.)** Don't you think Mr/Ms was a bit pathetic? **(Collect responses.)** How do you think he/she felt then? How frightened was he/she? **(Use the sliding scale and cartoon faces to register how frightened they think he/she was. Check with colleague.)** Are they right? I am sorry it was only a joke.

Here are some other things people are afraid of…

Watch the prepared mimes. After each one, pupils (a) guess what the situation was (b) decide how frightened the person was and come out to register it on the scale (c) say how they think the person felt (e.g. shaky, shivery, cold, clammy, wanting to cry).

(Accept the answers to show that all these responses are normal. If anyone laughs make it clear that for lots of people these are scary situations.)

Everyone is afraid sometimes and needs someone to help them feel safe. Who did Mr/Mrs call? It's OK to be afraid. **(Show frightened face and give thumbs up.)** Sailors on ships in storms feel afraid. They sometimes have to call for someone to make them safe. Who would they call? How could they do that? (flags, flare, radio)

(Hold up each emergency rescue symbol. Ask for each one.) If we called for help from here what might we be frightened of?

What kind of thing makes you feel afraid? Who could you call for help? (a teacher, parent or reliable adult, the police, Childline, a friend).

The green-eyed monster

Mirror mirror

YOU WILL NEED

A mirror, a flip chart, black, green and pink pens

(Hold up a mirror or draw one and look into it.) Have you ever thought how clever mirrors are? We can look into them and see ourselves. Have you ever played the game, where you pretend to be someone's reflection? *(Ask for a volunteer to be your reflection and copy your actions. If time, pairs of pupils can try or the whole audience can be your reflection.)* It's a good game isn't it? But no matter how good you are at copying someone, the two of you can never be exactly the same. Each person is different and special in their own way. *(Look into your mirror again, tidy your hair, then look away and sigh.)* The trouble is we don't always think of that when we look in the mirror. We often want the very opposite of what we are. If we are

short, we want to be tall. If we have long hair we want…If we have straight hair we want it to be …If we are skinny, we want to be…
Sometimes we wish we looked like a friend and we feel jealous. It can make us behave badly towards them. Do you remember the wicked queen in *Snow White*? *(Look in the mirror again and say 'Mirror, mirror on the wall, who is the fairest of them all?')* The queen was so jealous of Snow White she tried to get rid of her. Jealousy is sometimes called 'the green-eyed monster' because of the way it can make people behave. *(Draw a pair of large green eyes.)* When we look through these jealous eyes, we are never happy. *(Draw some pink spectacles.)* Luckily if we know the monster is about, we can put these on and make the jealousy go away. So next time you feel bad about yourself and jealous of someone, put on your magic glasses and try to think of something good about yourself instead.

Prayers and Thinking

Have you ever been jealous of someone? What were you jealous of? Was it how they looked, or something they could do and you couldn't? It's not a nice feeling is it? Try and see a picture of yourself feeling jealous. Now take that picture and tie it onto a balloon. Tie it really tight. Let the balloon go. Watch it float away, getting smaller and smaller, taking your picture and your bad feelings away too. Next time you feel jealous, you can do the same thing. Try to learn how to enjoy yourself and your friendships without feeling jealous.

 Quote for the day

O! beware, my lord, of jealousy! It is the green-eyed monster which doth mock the meat it feeds on.
Iago in *Othello*, William Shakespeare

Faith links

Christian and Jewish
Joseph's jealous brothers
Genesis 37: 3-11)

Branching out

 Make sets of pink spectacles to look through and practise saying something good about yourselves when you wear them!

 Carry out the idea for the prayer with real pictures and balloons.

 Read some of Aesop's fables with a similar theme. Try 'The Raven and the Swan' or 'The Vain Jackdaw'. Make up some fables of your own.

Birds of a feather

There was once an amazing forest. **(Pupils hold up leaves and flowers, play forest music.)** In the middle of the forest lived some birds so beautiful they were said to come from heaven; they were called 'Birds of Paradise'. The birds were very proud and spent a long time preening, so not even a speck of dust would soil their beauty. They posed high up in the trees, where everyone could see how beautiful they were. **(Birds enter, twirl and pose as if models, then stand and preen.)**

One very special tree was used each year to hold dancing competitions and to try and attract a wife. As the male birds strutted along the dancing branch, the female birds lined up in the other trees to watch; it was just like a catwalk at a fashion parade. **(All three birds parade up and down to music, females 'ooh' and clap.)** The males were vain and jealous of each other, each one wanting to be the best. The birds began to brag about who would win. **(Each bird takes it in turn to strut along as if on a catwalk, showing off their particular set of feathers under a spotlight.)**

The Golden Bird of Paradise was the first to walk along the branch. 'Look at my wonderful head-dress,' he called as he fluttered his feathers and bounced and danced his six golden head plumes in front of his eyes. 'Is that all!' the Greater Bird of Paradise laughed as he joined him on the branch. He threw his long side feathers into the air, becoming a fountain of yellow and pink. 'Ah, but look at me!' boasted the Magnificent Bird of Paradise pushing the others out of the way. He spread a wide golden cape over his shoulders, shaking and quivering the golden feathers to catch the sunlight.

As the three birds strutted and posed waiting for the female birds to choose, they began to worry. What if they weren't chosen? What if their feathers weren't good enough? Each bird began to look at the others and to doubt himself. **(Birds line up together and look anxiously at own feathers and at each other.)** Each wished it had the beauty of the other two. They began to try and push each other off the branch. **(Jostling and pushing.)**

They felt so jealous they pecked at each others feathers. **(Begin to lift and pull at each others feathers and then act out following scene.)** The Magnificent Bird of Paradise pulled out the head-dress of the Golden Bird of Paradise. The Golden Bird of Paradise plucked the fountain of the Greater Bird of Paradise and the Greater Bird of Paradise tore the cape of Magnificent Bird of Paradise. They were so jealous they just couldn't stop. Feathers and squawks filled the forest as the females looked on in horror. **(Loud squawking from all and feathers thrown.)**

Suddenly the trees fell quiet. Three completely plucked birds sat on the dancing branch. They had no feathers left at all! They shivered and huddled together to keep warm. **(Birds try to cover themselves with their hands as if naked.)** Soon all the females were laughing and pointing at them. Gathering some leaves to hide their shame, the featherless birds crept away. **(Hold up large leaves to hide their modesty.)** Hiding together in the depths of the forest, out of sight of prying eyes, they waited for new feathers to grow. Each, now much wiser bird, vowed never to let jealousy get the better of them again. **(Birds peep out from the leaves, play forest music.)**

Think fit

Refer to maker's instructions

YOU WILL NEED
Flip chart and marker pen

(Ask two or three pupils to come out and take off their cardigans/jumpers.)
See if you can find the labels that tell us how to look after them.
(Copy some of the wash care symbols onto the flip chart. Include a 'crossed out' symbol.) (Pupils sit down.)

(Indicate each symbol.) What does this symbol mean? Does it tell us to do something? Or does it tell us not to do something? *(Write meaning underneath symbol.)* Why is it there? (It might shrink/colour run.)

The symbols tell us what to do *(nod head, encourage pupils join in)* and they tell us what we shouldn't do. *(Shake head, pupils to join in.)* We are a bit like those jumpers, we need special care if we are to be healthy.

(New flip chart sheet.) (Head sheet 'Care label for me'. Draw large label outline.)

*What do we need to do to keep healthy? *(Take one suggestion – ask a pupil to mime.)* Is it something we should do *(nod)* or is it something we shouldn't do? *(Shake head.)* What symbol could we draw on our care label? *(Discuss and select – pupil draw on flip chart.)**

*(Repeat from * to * until a series of symbols are on the flip chart. Suggestions: exercise, clean teeth, eye tests. Include negatives, e.g. Do not smoke/take drugs/eat junk foods.)*

Let's look again at our care label and what the symbols tell us. If it tells us to **do** something, nod and shout 'yes' *(nod)* if it is something we **mustn't do**, shake your head and shout 'no'. *(Shake.) (Point to each symbol encourage response.)*

(To quieten down!) Let's begin now with some exercises. Stretch up *(all stretch arms up)* wriggle fingers. *(Wriggle.)* Stretch our neck *(turn head slowly from side to side)* relax our necks *(drop chin onto chest)* close our eyes to rest them. *(Close eyes.) (Go straight to praying and thinking.)*

Prayers and Thinking

(Ask staff to help any pupils unable to do this unaided, or twin with another pupil)
Some of you will want to offer this to God as a prayer... Stretch arms up to say thankyou for our bodies. Stretch arms out to be willing to help others. Stretch arms forward to say thankyou for those who help us when we are not healthy. Hands on knees, pray or think for a moment about someone you know who isn't healthy or well. Fold arms.

Quote for the day

Health is the second blessing that we mortals are capable of; a blessing that money cannot buy.
(Izaak Walton 1593-1683 – The Compleat Angler pt 1)

Faith links

Christan and Jewish
Naaman the leper
2 Kings 5

Branching out

 Design a care label for a friend.

 In groups, devise a set of exercises that can be done at your desk. Think of all parts of the body.

 Design a cartoon care leaflet for young children showing how to keep healthy.

Fit as a fiddle?

PREPARATION NEEDED

A pupil to be Tom in PE kit and sweatshirt, towel and shower gel

flip chart (divided into 2 columns with a ✓ at top of 1 and ✗ at top of 2)

marker pen

groups of pupils in PE kit to do different exercises to the refrain (*)

comfy chair

(optional – giant burger or take away box)

(Introduce Tom with towel over his shoulder and shower gel in his hand.) We are going to take Tom to the gym. He needs encouraging to do his exercises. Every time you hear the word **exercise,** you call out **'**Exercises, exercises, you must do your exercises'**. Let's practise…Tom had to do his **exercises.** **(*)** *(Practise a few times.)*

Tom really wanted to play for the local football team. The coach looked at him. 'You haven't been looking after yourself. You'll have to get fit and healthy before you can play a match,' he said. 'That means lots of **exercise** **(*)** *(groups exercise and say refrain)* and early nights.' 'I suppose that means I'll have to go to the gym,' muttered Tom 'I can fiddle it to look as if I'm doing something'

Off he went. There were lots of people doing **exercises (*)** Tom looked at the group doing arm stretches. **(Group of pupils do arm stretches.)** 'That looks the easiest **exercise** for me,' **(*)** he said, took off his sweatshirt and went to join the group. 'Don't forget to warm up first,' said one of the group. **(Tom rubs his arms and legs.)** Then he started his **exercises. (*) (Tom joins in half-heartedly.)** You can't fool us Tom. You won't get fit like that.

Tom's arms soon got tired. 'I'll exercise my legs now', he thought and went to join the group running on the spot **(group running)**. 'This is hard **exercise**,' he puffed. **(*)** 'I'm just going to pretend.' 'Don't forget to drink water while you're **exercising**,' **(*)** said one of the runners.

Tom was glad to stop for a drink. 'I'll do one more **exercise (*)** before I go home,' sighed Tom 'something not too hard. Waist twisting looks an OK **exercise'. (*) (Group waist twisting.)** After 5 minutes Tom had had enough. **(Tom stops, bends over puffing, looking as if he's done a lot.)**

'I need a shower,' he said to Tim, 'I'm so hot..' 'Make sure you put a warm top on afterwards,' said Tim, 'or your muscles will tighten up'. **(Tom mimes having shower, dries himself, puts on sweatshirt.)**

On the way home, Tom was starving 'All that **exercise (*) (all groups exercise)** has made me hungry,' he thought. He stopped at the Burger Bar and ordered a monster burger with double fries. He took them home and settled down to watch the late film. *(settles into comfy chair)*. At training the next day Tom was tired out. 'What about the early nights and **exercise**? **(*) (All groups exercise.)** You'll have to do better than this,' said the coach.

Tom wasn't trying very hard was he? He was pretending. What things did he do that would help him get healthy? **(List in column1 on flip chart.)** (Exercise, warm up, drank water, had a shower, put on warm clothing.) What unhealthy choices did Tom make? (Burger, late night.) **(List in column 2. Discuss why they're not healthy.)** There's something we need to tell Tom before we go. **(Groups say – Healthy choices, healthy choices, you must now make healthy choices.) (All pupils join in.)**

Lovin' proof...

Words of love...

YOU WILL NEED

Flip chart, marker pens, a Bible or large book, A colleague to fidget as you begin reading. An 'assistant' colleague with a photocopy of the assembly who will share the dialogue with you

Leader: (*Very serious! To pupils.*) Today we are going to learn about love. (Write LOVE IS ... at the top of flip chart.) I am going to read to you from the Bible. Please be quiet and listen carefully. (**Open Bible / book. Take a deep breath, read in an exaggerated way.**) Love is patient. (**Assistant writes 'Patient' on flip chart.**) (**Colleague fidgets.**)

Leader: (*Pause and speak impatiently.*) Mr/Ms ___ will you please settle down, I'm trying to teach this lot! **Assistant**: (**to pupils**) Is Mr/Mrs (leader) being very patient? (**Encourage negative response and pupils to give it a thumbs down.**)

Leader: Attention! Love is kind. (**Assistant writes on flip chart.**) (**Leader looks up and sniffs.**) Someone here is wearing perfume that smells like a drain. It's horrible! **Assistant:** Is that a kind thing to say? (**Thumbs down.**)

Leader: (*Exasperated.*) Love doesn't get jealous. (**Assistant writes 'not jealous' and looks at leader expectantly.**)

Leader: (*Thoughtful, with a fed up expression.*) You know I'd really like Mr/Ms ____'s coffee mug it's much smarter than mine. They don't deserve a smart coffee mug. **Assistant:** Do you think Mr/Mrs ___ is jealous of that coffee mug? (**Thumbs down.**)

Leader: (*to assistant*) Well if it breaks they're not borrowing mine!... Now where were we? (**Wagging finger at pupils.**) Love is not selfish. (**Assistant writes ' is not selfish'. Shakes head and pulls a face.**) (**Thumbs down.**) **Assistant:** (**To pupils.**) I'm not sure Mr/Mrs ___ is the best person to be telling us about love, are you? Shall we start again and show him/her how it's done?

Leader: That's fine by me but you're not having my book. **Assistant:** I think that's being selfish too! Now let me see ... .. (**Point to word on flip chart.**) Love is patient. What could Mr/Mrs (leader) have done to be loving and patient with Mr/Ms___ ? (**Encourage answers like, wait for them, ask if they are OK.**) (**Draw a heart by the word and give a thumbs up.**) (**Repeat for KIND, NOT JEALOUS.**) (**Point to 'IS NOT SELFISH'.**)

Leader: (*Butting in.*) Alright, I've got it. Mr/Ms____ can borrow my mug if they want to. **Assistant**: (**Encourage applause and give a thumbs up.**) (**Draw a heart on the corner of the flip chart, tear it off and give it to leader.**) So what is love like?

Prayers and Thinking

(*Draw a medium sized heart on the flipchart. Say...*) Feel your heart. (*Put hand on heart.*) Think about people you love and who love you. Think about times you are half-hearted (*draw a line across the middle*) and don't show them you love them. Or perhaps you do things that break their heart. (*Draw a zig-zag line from top to bottom.*) Ask God to help you, or make up your mind, to be big hearted (*Draw a big heart round the smaller one*) and always be loving.

Quote for the day

True love's the gift which God has given, To man alone beneath the heaven. Sir Walter Scott (1771–1832) *The Lay of the Last Minstrel* V:13

Faith links

Christian
The Crucifixion
Romans 5: 6-8

Jewish
David and Jonathan
1 Sam: 20

Branching out

 Write a 'love is ...' sentence and illustrate it

 Draw a heart, half a heart, a broken heart, big heart. Write words on them to describe that kind of person

 Cut out paper hearts and give them to people you love. Ask them to pass them on.

Have a heart!

Today's story is a love story. *('Aaah' encourage participation.) (Draw a heart in the middle of the flip chart.)* And I'm going to need help to tell it.

(Divide assembly into 5 groups. A pupil sits facing each group holding one of the hearts, 1 pupil sitting behind them with the big heart.) (Tell each group what they are.)

When you hear your heart mentioned jump up and sit down again. *(Practise each one. All jump up for 'big heart'. If this won't work, waving hands will be fine.)*

Story: Anna and Troy had been in love for ages *(Troy and Anna, with hats and dummies, come in holding hands)*; ever since the day they had been born at the same hospital. *(Write 'Anna loves Troy' on the heart, with an arrow through.)* As they grew up they were best friends. *(Skip round together.)*

Troy had a **soft heart.** *(Write soft heart at top of next page of flip chart.)* Does that mean Troy was a kind person? *(Write kind next to soft heart.)* Anna was a toughie and could be rather **hard-hearted.** *(Write hard heart.)* Was she as kind as Troy? *(Write could be unkind.)* However Troy loved her with his **whole heart. (Write whole heart.)** Did he love her a lot or a little bit? *(Write loved a lot.)* Do you know, he loved her even when she was **hard-hearted** and grabbed his toys and crawled away. *(Grabs Troy's toy and runs.) (Aaah.)*

When they were old enough they went to nursery. *(Remove woolly hats and dummies. Pick up lunch boxes.)* There Anna met Carl *(enter Carl)*, their eyes met and he won her heart. *(Hold hands and walk away from Troy.)* Anna and Carl played together all day, leaving Troy **broken-hearted.** *(Write broken hearted.)* Was Troy happy or sad? *(Write – sad)*

By the time they went to Primary school *(put down lunch boxes, pick up school bags)* Troy was feeling a bit fed up with Anna. 'Will you play with me?' she asked at breaktime, 'I don't know anyone else.' Troy looked to where his friends were playing football, he enjoyed kicking a ball around but he had noticed how unhappy Anna was at their new school. 'OK' he said. *(Aaah.)* 'That sounds **half-hearted,**' said Anna. *(Write half-hearted.)* Did Carl really want to play with Anna? *(Write didn't really want to.)* Why do you think he did? *(Encourage -because he was her best friend - because he loved her.)*

Everyday they walked to school together. Sometimes Troy carried Anna's bag, especially if it was heavy. *(Aaah.)* He had forgotten his **broken heart** and was **wholeheartedly**, enjoying being Anna's special friend again, although he would have liked to play with the others.

One day when they got to the playground Anna said 'Troy, why don't you go and play football, I can watch with the others.' 'That didn't sound **half-hearted,**' thought Troy, 'maybe Anna's **hard heart** has changed to a **soft heart**'. Troy didn't need to be told twice, he was off playing with the team. When the bell went Troy ran over to Anna 'Thanks'' he said, 'That was very **big-hearted'.**

(Write big-hearted on the flip chart.) Anna has changed. *(Give Anna the big heart.)* Is she better or worse now? What is different? Who helped her change? Why? (*Because he loved her –*

Where there's a will...

Holding on

YOU WILL NEED

A flip chart, a pen and a pair of scissors

(Write the word 'Patience' in large letters.) Our assembly is all about this word. Does anyone know what it is? What does it mean? It isn't easy to be patient. It can be hard to keep on trying to do something when it takes a long time, if it's painful or difficult. It is much easier to give up and stop trying or to get cross about it. What do you think 'losing your patience' means? Is it like this? **(Cut out the word patience and walk round with it, pretend to drop it on the floor and lose it. Walk round the room saying crossly 'Oh no! I've really lost my patience now!')** What sort of things make you lose your patience?

Have you ever heard anyone say 'He was really stretching my patience.' What do you think that means? How could we show the meaning with our word? **(Invite volunteers to demonstrate, prompt them to mime stretching the word.)** Who can tell us about when their patience has been stretched?

What about 'My patience is wearing out'? **(Ask for another volunteer, prompt them to rub, fold, and crumple the word so that it looks tatty and worn.)**

Sometimes, staying patient is so hard to do, that people finally lose their temper and their 'patience snaps'. **(Ask for a volunteer to demonstrate this by pulling the word in two.)** Has your patience ever snapped? What happened?

(Hold up snapped patience.) Oh dear! I think we need more patience than this. **(Write the word again.)** This time lets try hard not to let our patience snap. We'll keep calm and 'hold onto our patience' even when it's stretched. **(Two volunteers mime this.)** Well done. You really 'held onto' your patience didn't you? It is possible to 'keep your patience' after all. **(Applaud and give a pupil patience to keep.)**

Can you keep yours?

Prayers and Thinking

The gentle gifts that patience brings are calmness and peace.

May your heart and mind feel these gentle gifts…

Calmness and peace…

Calmness and peace…

(Leave space for stillness or quietly play a 'rain maker' to emulate the sound of the sea)

Quote for the day

He that has patience may compass anything.
François Rabelais (1490–1553) *Works*, Book IV, Ch xlviii

Faith links

Christian
The patience of love, 1 Corinthians 13: 4-7

Sikh
Rama, Jetha and the seven platforms

Branching out

 Use containers and pebbles to test what Crow did (see p. 61). Does it work? Does the size and shape of the stones and container make a difference? Which combination needs the most patience?

 Visit www.rnid.org. uk Learn to finger spell the word patience. Now teach it to someone else who doesn't know finger spelling. Were you a patient teacher?

 Write or act out your own fable to show the meaning of 'It was enough to test the patience of a saint.'.

The thirsty crow

PREPARATION NEEDED

The assembly leader needs to learn the signs beforehand! See Appendix 1, p. 131.

A set of line drawings or rebus symbols to represent each sign

WHAT TO DO

Show the signs to the audience before telling the story. Once is enough, as there is plenty of time to practise during the story!

Read the story and sign the words that are highlighted.

Use facial expressions as you sign to emphasise meaning and feelings.

Say the highlighted words slightly louder to draw attention to the need to sign.

Go slowly – so that the audience has time to join in.

I'm going to use sign language to help me tell a story. You can do the signs too. Some of you might know them already. Let's practise the signs we will need. **(Show pictures, ask audience what they stand for. Demonstrate signs and audience copies.)**

Today's story was written by a man called Aesop. All his stories have a message for people to think about. See if you can work out what this one is. It is called 'The Thirsty Crow'. When you hear the words we have practised, try and sign with me.

It was a very **HOT** day. The **SUN** beat down and dried up all the **WATER** in the puddles – until there was **NONE LEFT**. All the **BIRDS** had to **FLY** to the **RIVER** to get a **DRINK**. It was such a long way to **FLY**. They got very **TIRED** and **THIRSTY**.

CROW was so **TIRED** of **FLYING**. He was sure he'd never **(shake head)** make it to the **RIVER**. Many of the other **BIRDS** had got so **TIRED** they had **DROPPED** from the sky. **CROW** worried that he might be next and so he stopped for a **REST**.

The **SUN** got **HOTTER** and **HOTTER**. **CROW** got **THIRSTIER** and **THIRSTIER**. He didn't know what to do! **(Shrug and shake head.)**

Just then, he saw a **BUCKET**. When he hopped over to have a closer look, you'll never guess what was **IN** the **BUCKET**! Yes **WATER**, but only a very **LITTLE** bit, right at the bottom!

Poor **CROW** couldn't **(shake head)** reach the **WATER** with his beak. **(Point to beak.)** But what he did next was very clever. He picked up a **STONE** and **DROPPED** it **INSIDE** the **BUCKET**. Then he got another **STONE** and **DROPPED** it **INSIDE** the **BUCKET**, and another and another and another. Then something very exciting began to happen. Each time **CROW DROPPED** a **STONE IN** the **BUCKET**, the **WATER** moved up and up **(mime water as you move hand upwards)** and up.

CROW kept on **DROPPING STONES** for a very long time. He got so **TIRED**, but he never gave up. **(Shake head.)** He kept on and on until the **WATER** reached the very top of the **BUCKET**.

Then a very **THIRSTY** but happy **CROW** reached down **INTO** the lovely cool **WATER** and **DRANK** and **DRANK** and **DRANK**!

Crow got a lovely drink in the end didn't he? Did you manage all the signs? Did you keep on going? What do you think the message of this story is? Were you like Crow?

A sad state of affairs

Sadness A-Z

YOU WILL NEED

Flip chart, marker pens, plain paper, scissors, Blu-Tack

(Write these words across the top of the flip chart as the pupils are assembling – miserable, glum, down in the dumps, unhappy, heartbroken, sorrowful, blue, tearful, woeful.)

Just look at these words. (If younger pupils or those with language difficulties are present, comment jokingly.) They are very long words aren't they, but listen and see if you can say them with me.

(Point to first word.) Can anyone help me read this word? *(Repeat the word clearly and pull a sad face.)* *(Praise anyone who has a go even if they are wrong.)* Now you say it with me. *(Repeat for all the words.)*

We are going to write these words in an alphabetical list. Let's have a go at saying the alphabet first. *(All recite alphabet.)*

What's the first letter of the alphabet? *(Point to flip chart.)* Can anyone show us a word beginning with A? What's the next letter then? (B) Is there a word beginning with B? *(Ask pupil to come out and point to the word, you say it and write it at the top of a list. Work through the alphabet in this way until the list is complete.)*

What do you think all these words mean? *(Take ideas, if struggling say...)* Watch my face. *(Pull sad face.)* All those long words mean SAD. *(Write Sad across the bottom of the flip chart in large letters with a sad face.)* What sort of things make us sad? *(Take ideas without comment.)*

We organised those words into alphabetical order easily didn't we? But when we feel sad about something it isn't always easy to sort it out and feel happy again. Sometimes we need to have a good cry or be with a friend or just be on our own. Next time you're sad, think what you want to do and ask someone to help.

Prayers and Thinking

(OPTIONAL – small container of water and bowl) (Cut out three or four tear shapes and give to pupils Say...)

___ -, ___-, ___- and ___ will come and stick the tears down the flip chart. As they stick each one, think about something or someone that makes you feel sad. We will then close our eyes and be quiet. (Listen as I pour the water.) Think about the tears dropping onto the ground and soaking away taking your sadness with them. At the same time, those who pray, can ask God to take away your sadness and help you be happy. *(Slowly pour water.)*

Quote for the day
He who conceals his grief finds no remedy for it. (Turkish proverb)

Faith links

Christian
The Resurrection, Mary at the tomb
John 20

All faiths
Funeral rites

Branching out

 Make a display of tear shapes falling onto the ground. Write on each, something that makes you sad. Draw shoots, of words, coming up from the ground that are a positive result of tears, e.g. peace, hope, friendship, sharing, understanding.

 Find as many words as possible linked to sadness. Place them along a 'sadness scale'.

 Draw a picture or write a description of something you would be sad to lose.

The tissue trail

PREPARATION NEEDED

Flip chart with a sad face at the top

marker pens

sadness scale(see p. 23) (or draw on flip chart)

3 pupils to mime being '3 degrees of sad' with a 'sad' mask each

3 chairs

3 'buddies' sitting in their normal seat with an empty seat next to them

a box of tissues

WHAT TO DO

Before the Assembly, take the tissues out of the box keeping them in a pile. Begin with the top tissue, unfold and write a large S. On the next A, and on the next D. Continue with TEARFUL and UNHAPPY. Refold and put back in the box, in order.

(As you greet the assembly, three pupils walk in looking very sad / crying / wailing.) Goodness you look really upset, what's the matter? **(They don't stop)** Has something happened? **(Go from one to the other not knowing how to stop them.)** Come and sit down. Let's see if we can help you.

(Ask assembly) They all look very sad, who do you think is the saddest? **(Ask why they think that – because of the noise etc. Write the names along the sadness scale.)**

(Ask all three, who shake heads to each question) Have you hurt yourselves? Do you feel sick? Are you in trouble? Have you been told off? Have you had a quarrel? **(Getting more puzzled.)**

(*Pick up the box of tissues and ask someone to pull one out and give it to the 1st sad pupil to wipe their eyes. Shake it, look surprised.) That's no good it's got writing on it. **(Hold it up. Ask what the letter is (S). Ask someone else to pull out the next tissue. Same thing happens (A) then (D). When SAD is out of the box, read the word together.)**
(Pupil 1 jumps up nodding his/her head)

Are you feeling SAD? **(Pupil nods.)** Do you want to tell us why?
We played a football match last night and we lost. **(Hold up sad mask)**
(Assembly respond aaah.)

I hear you all played really well so I understand you're disappointed. Perhaps you will win the next game..
(Ask another pupil to be their buddy for the day to cheer them up. Pupil 1 sits down feeling a bit better.) *

*(Turn to pupil 2. Repeat from * to * substituting TEARFUL – because they have lost something special to them.)*

*(Turn to pupil 3. Repeat from * to * substituting UNHAPPY – because someone / pet has died, is ill, is going away, etc.)*

(Recap. Indicate the three words and scale)
_____ was feeling SAD because _____.
(Assembly to recall.) _____ was feeling TEARFUL because _____ . _____ was feeling UNHAPPY because _____.

They were all feeling? .... **(point to SAD on flip chart)** because they had lost something.

We all feel sad sometime. That's OK. What do we need when we are sad? **(A friend or buddy)**

(Ask buddies to come and take their pupil to sit down in the Assembly.)

'You are...' 'I am?!'

What am I worth?

YOU WILL NEED

A pupil to mime Sally, leader is Ali. Flip chart divided into 2 across the middle, marker pens, 4 sheets plain A4 paper, Blu-Tack **or** sticky tape

(My name is Ali, this is my friend Sally.) 'I'm useless,' moaned Sally to Ali, 'I can't buy Kay a birthday present because I've got no money. I'm poor and I'm a useless friend.' *(Ask how Sally is feeling. All make relevant facial expressions. Write ideas on top half of flip chart.)* Ali was cross 'You're not poor,' he exclaimed, 'just think of all you've got.' 'You tell me!' snapped Sally.

* Well, what about your **hands**? How much do you think Picasso's (or artist being studied) hands were worth? *(Draw a hand on sheet of paper, ask for values – explain he needed them to earn a living, write value by the hand, pupil holds up paper.)* 'Your hands must be worth something' *(Discuss what we use our hands for and how valuable they are.)**

Repeat from * to * using: feet – David Beckham, voice – name of current pop group, ears – Mozart

'There,' said Ali 'you're not poor, you're worth a lot.' 'I suppose I am,' said Sally looking at her hands and feet. 'But that doesn't help me give Kay a birthday present.' 'Think about it,' said Ali, 'You've got two arms **(hold out Sally's arms)** you could give her a hug and you've got a lovely smile **(encourage Sally to smile)** you could give her that too.'

(Ask assembly.) What other things could Sally give Kay as a present? (e.g. **time** – go for a walk, **skills** – make a special card, **share her things** – invite her home to listen to CDs, etc).

That's what Sally did. She made a card and on her birthday went to Kay's house. *(Choose a pupil to be Kay.)* When Kay opened the door, Sally gave her the card with a big hug and a smile. 'Happy birthday Kay, shall we walk into town to look at the shops and then go to my house to listen to CDs?' Kay was so excited. 'That's the best present I've had,' she laughed, 'I'm all on my own. How did you know what to do for my birthday? You are a really good friend!'

(Ask assembly.) How does Sally feel now? *(Write on bottom half of flip chart, make facial expressions.)*

(Ask pupils to put up their hands if they could – go for a walk, make a card, give a hug, etc.) Well we aren't poor and useless are we! We're very valuable.

Prayers and Thinking

(Draw a 'think bubble' on the flip chart. Say...) Think of yourself and how valuable you are. *(Draw another bubble.)* Think of something you are good at and be glad for that. Give yourself a hug because you are special. While you do that, if you'd like to pray, you can say thank you to God for making you special. Imagine He is giving you a hug too.

Quote for the day

Pooh's mind went back ... everybody had admired him so much; ... that didn't happen often... he would like it to happen again.
A A Milne (1928) *The House at Pooh Corner*

Faith links

Christian
Jesus's attitude to children
Mark 10: 13

All faiths
Initiation ceremonies

Branching out

 In groups, first person holds a ball. Everyone in the group says something positive about that person. Repeat for everyone. Each hold the ball again, repeat something said <u>about</u> you.

 Role play choosing teams for a game. Discuss how it feels to be the first/last to be chosen.

 Design a set of praise stickers to award in your class.

Marshmallow munchers

PREPARATION NEEDED

A bag of large marsmallows

think bubbles with compliments written on them

5-6 volunteers

flip chart and marker.

WHAT TO DO

Set up a row of 5–6 pupils, sitting on chairs, heads down, facing the assembly, each with a prepared answer to your question. Standing behind each one, a pupil with a think bubble.

Leader: What we say to others is important. We can say things to make each other feel good, but sometimes for one reason or another, although we think them, we don't say them. Let's see what happens.

(Introduce row of pupils.) Are they looking happy and pleased with themselves? I wonder what's the matter. *(Ask each one.)* What's the matter _____? *(Each replies with some negative feeling about themselves, e.g. I'm no good at games, I never get picked / No-one plays with me / My hair always looks a mess / I wish I could afford 'cool' trainers / I'm rubbish at... etc.)*

I think something could be said to make them feel better about themselves. Have you got any thoughts? *(Write ideas on speech bubbles on flipchart.) (Steer ideas towards the positive; 'Tell them something good about themselves.' Explain, saying 'It doesn't matter' isn't good enough. It does matter to them.)*

(While you are discussing this, the pupils standing behind the chairs hold up their think bubble, blank side facing the assembly.) (Name the pupils.) __, __, etc have

some thoughts on the matter. Let's see what they are.

(Ask for volunteer to come out and read the 1st think bubble. 1st think bubble is turned round. It should be relevant to what the person on the chair said. As the volunteer goes to read it, put a marshmallow in their mouth so the words are muffled. Thank them and tell them to sit down. Pupil sitting, remains head down.)

(Repeat for each speech bubble.)

Did that help? Why not? (e.g. they couldn't hear.) We need to say good things to people so they can hear. It's no use just thinking it or saying it to other people.
What could we do to help ___, ___, etc? (e.g. say it so they can hear.) Let's all do it together. *(Point to each think bubble, all read out loud. Pupil on chair lifts up head, smiles and gives thumbs up or some indication of feeling better about themselves.)*

Well that worked. Today, don't be a marshmallow mumbler, look for good things you can say to people and say them loud and clear.

True or False?

Crocodile tears

YOU WILL NEED
Place the script on a stand for this one

Long ago Crocodile lived in a river. He liked to lie in the water with just his eyes and nostrils poking out. **(Stretch out arms and claw hands together at the end as if closed teeth.)** He looked just like a bit of wood, floating on the water. Well until he smiled, **(open arms and fingers slightly)** for he had a mouth full of very large sharp teeth. And pieces of wood don't have teeth do they? Crocodile used to smile a big toothy smile at everyone that went by. The other creatures saw his smile and thought he was their friend.

Crocodile spent each day, floating very still …until he felt hungry. Then when nobody was watching, it was open… **(open arms wide clawing fingers as teeth)** snatch… **(close arms quickly)** down the hatch… **(arms down towards stomach)**. Crocodile would then lie still again as if nothing had happened. **(Whistle.)** But something had happened hadn't

it? **(Repeat this sequence with the audience joining in if they wish.)**

One day Crocodile was feeling a little peckish when a lovely tasty FISH came by. **(Make fish with hand.)** Crocodile checked to see that no one was watching… then … **(narrator and audience)** open, snatch, down the hatch… it was gone. **(Whistle.)** Later that night the FISH'S friends came looking for it. 'Isn't it sad that your friend is missing,' cried crocodile as a tear fell from his eye. **(Run a finger down your face.)**

Repeat story, for a FROG – jumping action with hand, a BIRD – flapping action, and RABBIT – ears on head.

Well, it didn't take too long for the animals to realise what was going on. 'We're not fooled by you,' they said. 'You're not really our friend. Those aren't real tears. Real tears fall from a truthful heart.' And from that day on they all knew crocodile tears when they saw them. Do you?

Prayers and Thinking

Have you ever told a lie? Do you always tell the truth?

Lies can make you feel all knotted and tied up inside. Telling the truth often makes you feel better

In the Bible it says that 'truth will make you free'.

Think about what this means to you.

Quote for the day
Truth is the cry of all, but the game of few.
George Berkeley, Irish Philosopher and Cleric (1685-1753) *Siris 368*

Faith links

Christian
Peter denies knowing Jesus Matthew: 26, 69–75

Buddhist
Four Noble Truths

Branching out

 How many words can you find that mean untruthful? Write them inside crocodile tears. Write truthful words inside true hearts. Talk about truth and lies.

 Make up some statements about topical stories in the news. Sort the statements into true and false.

 Make spirit levels out of junk materials. Some hardware stores supply 'screw in' bubbles, or use alternatives such as marbles or table tennis balls. How easy is it to be sure of a 'true' level?

On the level

PREPARATION NEEDED

Two members of staff, one who has put their watch one hour forward, the other one hour back.

assorted cardboard clock faces that can be altered

Blu-Tack

a large spirit level

a selection of smaller spirit levels (optional)

a long piece of wood

8 house bricks

hard hats (optional)

Good morning everyone, *(look at your watch)* has anyone got the time? I want to check that my watch is accurate, that it really is the time that it says it is. *(Accept times given by pupils but also include the staff members who have agreed to join in. As each time is given, invite pupils to the front to change a cardboard clock to that time. Attach the clocks to a flip chart.)* Hang on a minute! That can't be right! *(Look at all the clocks and begin to get exasperated by the different times their faces say.)* They can't all be true can they? It's hard to know which clock is right. The problem is you can change what they say so easily. You just move the hands at the back. When I look at each clock face; it looks like it's telling the truth. But some of them can't be; they must be lying! I don't know which clock to trust!

I do have something with me this morning that always tells the truth. *(Hold up a spirit level.)* Do you know what this is? Who might use one of these? What is it used for? That's right; it's used by builders or people doing DIY. It helps them tell if what they are making is 'on the level'. It helps them check if this level is 'true'. *(Draw a spirit level on the flip chart and point to the bubble. If you have time, pass round a few spirit levels for pupils to look at.)* You can tell when something is on the level, or when it is 'true', because the bubble is in the middle. If the bubble is not in the middle, the level is not true. It's as simple as that.

For example, if you are making a shelf to put some books on, *(hold up a piece of wood)* it needs to be level, like this for the books to stand on. If the shelf isn't level, like this *(slant the wood)* the books fall off. I'll show what you I mean. *(Put on hard hat.)* I'll need two helpers. *(Give them hard hats too.)* I want you to put

these bricks on top of each other at this side of a table. *(Pass the first helper three bricks.)* And I want you to put these bricks at the other side of the table. *(Pass the second helper four bricks.)* Now for the shelf! *(Place a piece of wood across the table, each end resting on a pile of bricks.)* How does that look? What do you mean it looks wonky? It looks alright to me! Tell you what; we'll get the spirit level to check if it's level. It'll soon tell us the truth. *(Use spirit level.)* Oh no! You're right! The bubble isn't in the middle, something must be wrong. What shall we do? *(You will soon be told how to correct the level, either by adding or removing a brick. Depending on the time you have available, you can either help or hinder the process by adding or removing bricks, or placing some bricks horizontally and others vertically. But eventually with the audience's help you will manage to get the wood level!)* Hey I think we've done it. Yes the bubble is in the middle. Our new shelf is on the level! Well done everyone!

Wasn't it useful to have a spirit level? It felt good to have something we could trust. Something we could rely on to tell us the truth. Is truth important to you? People can be a bit like spirit levels and clocks. Some feel that telling the truth is important. They try to be truthful, because they feel it's the right thing to do. It's like they have their own spirit level inside them. Other people know that they can trust them. But it's not always easy to tell the truth. Sometimes it's easier to be like the clocks we saw earlier, and change the truth to suit ourselves, just like when we changed the clock faces. Sometimes it's easier to lie. But is it the right thing to do? How can people trust someone who lies? What do you think? What sort of person do you want to be?

Value added

What's it worth?

YOU WILL NEED
Assorted coins, notes, cheque book, pen, Blu-Tack and a flip chart.

Tip the coins and notes onto a table. Can the children identify them? Explain that there are different types of money, and some coins and notes have a higher value than others. With the children's help, put the money in order from least valuable to the most valuable. Blu-Tack them to a flip chart and write their values underneath. **(Make sure there is room to add further items past the final one.)**

It is not only coins or notes that have value. Do you know what this is? **(Hold up a cheque book.)** When someone writes a cheque, it's like making a promise. The person who writes the cheque promises to pay another person the amount of money that they write down. They have to keep that promise and pay up! Even though the cheque is only a piece of paper, it has value because of the promise. **(Stick a blank cheque on the flip chart.)**

But it is not only money and cheques that have value. We have our own personal values too. These are often much more important to us than money. **(Write 'personal values' after the last item on the flip chart.)**

Our personal values are the things we think are important for living a 'good life.' For example, 'to be kind and not hurt people', or 'it is important to tell the truth'. We try to live our lives following these values, a bit like keeping a promise or writing a cheque to ourselves. **(Write one of the above promises on a cheque.)** Of course in real life, we don't have a cheque book to write our personal values in. We keep them inside ourselves instead. It's a bit like having our own cheque book of promises in our heads that we use to live our lives.

Prayers and Thinking

A famous preacher called John Wesley wrote a prayer about values. Listen to the prayer. Do you believe in the same values?

Do all the good you can.

By all the means you can.

In all the ways you can.

In all the places you can.

At all the times you can.

To all the people you can.

As long as ever you can.

Amen.

Quote for the day

It is our choices, Harry, that show what we truly are, far more than our abilities.
Dumbledore in JK Rowling (1998) *Harry Potter and the Chamber of Secrets*

Faith links

Christian
The ten commandments
Exodus 19: 20

Muslim
Muhammad's sayings in the Hadith

Branching out

 Make 'swingometers' with contradicting values at each end, e.g. love and hate, truth and lies, giving and taking, etc. Discuss the values and decide where the pointer should point.

 In groups, pupils make up their own manifestos and decide on a party name, slogan and logo. They can then present their party and its ideas to the rest of the class.

 Make a list of five personal values that you think are really important. Make a cheque book for the values with each value on a separate cheque written out to you.

Election Special

PREPARATION NEEDED

4 manifestos as described in the assembly (one blank) attached to a clip board

4 seats in a row with a carrier bag on each one

bag one – a rosette and logo for the Teddy Bear Party, a teddy bear, jar of honey

bag two – a rosette and logo for the Party Party, party hat, streamers and a party popper or whistle

bag three – a rosette and logo for the Pink Party, pink hat, pink flowers and a large paintbrush

bag four – a rosette and logo for the CBB Party, (no other items should be inside)

a further rosette with the school logo and name on it

WHAT TO DO

Presenter takes role of reporter with microphone

Another member of staff as CBB candidate

3 pupils as other candidates

Welcome to Election News Special. There are only a few more days to go until the election. Do you know who all the candidates are? Do you know what they believe? What are their values? Well, today, hot from the campaign trail we have some of the party leaders in school. They have come to tell us what is important to them and why we should vote for their party. Let's find out what they can do to make the world a better place.

I am now going to call on each leader to talk to you. Could we have the leader of the first party please… the Teddy Bear party. *(Party Leader goes to his/her seat, puts on rosette, shows items and shakes hands with the reporter. Introduces self to the audience and says 'I want everyone to vote for the Teddy Bear Party.')* The next candidate is the leader of the Party Party. *(Same routine.)* Next we have the leader of the Pink Party.' *(Same routine.)* Finally we have the leader of the…CBB Party. *(Nobody stands up.)* …err let me just check my notes, no there doesn't seem to be a name here or anything…The CBB party …I don't even know what CBB means. *(Opens bag and holds up rosette.)* I wonder who this belongs to? *(Selected member of staff shouts out… 'Well, it belongs to me actually. I was going to come and talk to everyone… but you see I can't be bothered.')* Well that isn't very good is it? Just a minute I get it…CBB stands for Can't Be Bothered doesn't it? You must be the leader of the Can't Be Bothered Party. *('Yes that's right but I can't be bothered to do anything about it.')* Oh well, I'll just leave your rosette here then.

Now we've got all the leaders here, it's going to be very important to listen to what they believe. Let's look at their manifestos. Remember a manifesto says what will make the world a better place. The first one says it wants to have …picnics in the woods and honey for tea… *(Ask the audience who they think it belongs to and then take it to the party leader for the Teddy Bear Party who says 'Vote Teddy Bear'.)* The next one says it is important to have all night parties and plenty of jelly. *(Same routine.)* This one says it will paint all houses pink and its slogan is 'Vote Pink or you stink!' *(Same routine.)* Now this last one says… (Turn the paper over) well there's nothing on it. *(Voice from other teacher: 'I couldn't be bothered to think of anything.')*

(News reporter turns to audience.) Now I don't think I've heard of anything so stupid in all my life. And as for the others…if they really think that picnics and parties and pink houses are the important things in life…well I feel sorry for them, don't you? They're just thinking of themselves. I'm not voting for any of them. Think of all the problems there are in the world today like war, and people with no homes or not enough food to eat. What we need is a party that has proper values. A party that believes in helping other people, now that would make a real difference.

I tell you what. What if there was another party. A 'name of school' Party? *(Hold up rosette.)* I bet that would be one to vote for. I'm sure all of you could think of some things that it could do to help people, don't you? *(You can choose to end here and move to the prayer/reflection, or you can ask for ideas and create an alternative manifesto in this or a further assembly.)*

Others

Do unto others...

Some things won't undo...

YOU WILL NEED

Flip chart, pen, paper, scissors, Sellotape

Do you know the story of Cinderella and her ugly sisters? What sort of things did the sisters do to Cinderella? They really meant to do nasty things didn't they? They were cruel. *(Write 'cruel' on a flip chart.)* Being cruel means doing horrid things to hurt other people even when you know it will upset them. Do you know of any other characters in stories that are cruel? What did they do? Of course cruelty doesn't only happen in stories, it can happen in real life too.

The trouble with cruelty is that it hurts so much. *(Write 'happy' on a flip chart and draw a happy face at the side.)* Do you think if someone has been cruel to you, it makes you feel happy inside? No, it makes you feel UNhappy. *(Add prefix UN to happy and change the face.)* Write 'loved' and draw a heart at the side. Do you think if someone has been cruel to you, you feel loved? No, it makes you feel UNloved. *(Add prefix and a cross over the heart.)*

Not only does cruelty hurt, it is very hard to forget. It can be something that is quite quick and easy to do *(write 'do')* but once it is done, it is difficult to UNdo. *(Add UN.)* Let me show you what I mean. Some things are easy to undo. I can fold my arms and then UNfold them. I can cross my legs and UNcross them. I can bend and UNbend. But cruelty isn't like that. If we take this piece of paper and screw it up. *(Ask volunteer.)* We can try and smooth it out again *(volunteer)* but we can still see the creases. If it is cut into pieces *(volunteer)* and then we try to stick it back together again, *(volunteer and Sellotape)* we can still see and more importantly feel all the cuts we made *(pass round)*

Cruelty is like that. It lasts for a long time and is difficult to forget. If you are ever tempted to be cruel – don't. Remember you can't UNhit, you can't UNtease, you can't UNpush. Even if you can't see what you have done, it can still be felt for a long time to come.

Prayers and Thinking

Write the words 'UNkind' 'UNfriendly' 'UNhelpful' and 'UNfair' on strips of paper. Invite children to come and hold them up. Remind everyone how hurtful these are.

Instead of being unkind to others we should try our best to be kind. Cut off the 'UN.' Do the same with each word then read them.

Sit quietly and think about how we can be more like these words. If you want to, you can say a prayer that asks for help and comfort for anyone you know that has suffered cruelty in their lives. Amen

Quote for the day

Cruelty has a human heart...
William Blake (1757–1827) Appendix to the Songs of Innocence and of Experience, 'A Divine Image'

Faith links

Christian
The cruelty of Herod
Matthew 2: 16

Buddhist
Following 'The Middle Path' and 'Right Action'

Branching out

 Make two ugly sister silhouettes for the wall and display 'cruel' words around it. Then make a fairy godmother silhouette with 'kind' words.

 Look at how adding and removing the suffix 'UN' can change the meaning of words, e.g. un/kind, un/fair, un/friendly, un/feeling, un/helpful.

 Cut, tear, crumple, fold, and shred coloured paper to create a collage of the word 'cruelty'.

The wind of change

PREPARATION NEEDED

Two ugly sister masks on sticks (these can be made quite quickly from paper plates)

shooting star on a stick

a member of staff prepared to have something stolen from them

one or two members of staff to help encourage audience participation and sound effects

this assembly can either be narrated by the assembly leader playing both parts by exchanging masks! Or it can be acted out with a partner or by volunteers from the audience. You might like to practise the sound effects with the audience first!

There was once a group of travellers who moved from town to town putting on shows. When they put on 'Cinderella' the actors who played the ugly sisters wore masks to help them look the part. 'Pickonyou' was the oldest. **(Hold mask up to face.) I am the most beautiful woman in the world** Audience**: Oh no you're not!** Pickonyou**: Oh yes I am!** 'Meanitricks' was the youngest. **(Hold up mask.) They're right, you're not the most beautiful; I am!** Audience**: Oh no, you're not!** Meanitricks**: Oh yes, I am.** In the pantomime, Pickonyou and Meanitricks had to pretend to be cruel to Cinderella. Pickonyou had to pick on Cinderella, making her do all the dirty work, and say horrid things to make her cry. 'Meanitricks' had to play nasty tricks on Cinderella, like throwing her washing in the mud, and laughing when she got upset. In fact, they were so good at pretending to be cruel the audience booed and hissed when they came on. **(Hold up masks, audience boos.)** The trouble was they got so good at pretending to be cruel, they found it hard to stop when the show was over. Pickonyou carried on picking on the other actors, shouting at them when they walked by her caravan. **(Hold up mask and shout at audience.) Here, are you looking in my windows?** and **Don't you walk near my wagon, I'll have you**… **(Shakes fist, audience boos.)** And as for Meanitricks, well she just couldn't stop her meanness. **(Hold up mask, audience boos.)** She played horrid tricks on everyone. **(Run over and take something from a member of staff, hide it behind your back and refuse to give it back. Laugh when they pretend to get upset.) (Stop and put down mask.)** One night,

Pickonyou and Meanitricks had been so cruel to everyone after the show that some of them began to think about leaving. They sat round the camp fire and talked about how they couldn't stand it any more. As they looked out into the night, they saw a star whiz across the sky. **(Audience whizzes.)** They knew the old story that shooting stars could make wishes come true. So what do you think they wished for? Well, whatever it was, that night something strange happened. A wind of change blew through the camp **(audience blows)**, rattling the branches of the trees and tapping at the windows of the wagons. **(Audience taps on chairs.)** In the morning, when everyone looked out, they could see Pickonyou and Meanitricks in the middle of the field, pulling at their faces. Somehow their masks had got stuck and they couldn't take them off! Each time they looked at each other for help, they were cruel to each other instead. **This is all your fault!** shouted Meanitricks at Pickonyou. **Oh shut up!** whined Pickonyou as she ran round and kicked her on the bottom. This carried on all day until the two were exhausted. They sat down on the grass as night began to fall. **It's not very nice to be picked on,** cried Pickonyou. **It's not very nice to have mean tricks played on you either,** cried Meanitricks. **If only our masks would come off**, the two wept. **We would never be cruel again!** And just at that moment, as luck would have it, a shooting star whizzed by **(audience whizzes)**, the wind of change returned **(blowing)**, rattling the trees and tapping at the windows of the wagons **(tapping)**… I wonder what happened next…

A little understanding

Every picture tells a story

YOU WILL NEED
Flip chart, pen, scissors

Have you ever looked at the work of famous artists? There is a famous painting of a lady called *Mona Lisa* by Leonardo da Vinci. People say that the smile on her face 'follows you about the room'. **(Draw a smile, cut it out, walk round making the smile follow you.)** Do you think it really does? Another famous painting by Picasso called *The Weeping Woman* shows a woman who is so sad that it looks like her face is cracking and falling to pieces. **(Draw sad/cracking face.)** Real faces don't, do they?

But we can tell how people are feeling by looking at their faces, can't we? Just like an artist does when painting a picture, when he or she tries to draw how that person is feeling. This morning, we're going to make our own gallery of portraits. These are the picture frames. **(Draw four different ones.)** All we need now are the pictures to go inside.

This is going to be a picture called Happy Harry. **(Write title under frame.)** How can I show that he is happy? Can anyone help me by pulling a happy face that I can copy? Just a minute, I think we need a frame for that. **(Cut out centre of a piece of paper to leave a large frame for the volunteer to look through. Begin to draw.)** This is quite tricky; can someone else come and help get it right? **(Finish picture together, checking that you have a smile, no frown, etc.)** The next one is called Angry Arthur. **(Repeat process, for angry, sad and scared, adding names to the portraits as you go.)** In comic books, artists sometimes add sound effects. If someone's tired they put 'yawn' in a speech bubble. What sound might Happy Harry make? **(Add Ha, ha/tee-hee, etc. Repeat process for others, sad—Boo hoo/sniff sniff, angry—Bah/Grrr! Scared—Eeek, arrgh!)**

If the people in these pictures were real, what would you think and do if you saw them? Do you think any of them need our help? What should we do? The people around us are just like this gallery. If we look closely and listen to what they say, we might be able to understand and help them when they need us.

Prayers and Thinking

You will need a flip chart and pen

(Read the poem below, drawing a question mark in the middle, with a pair of eyes, ears, lips and hands around it.)

Do you know what it takes to understand?
Eyes to see,
Ears that hear,
Words of comfort,
And a helping hand.

Let's think and pray about someone who needs our understanding today.

 Quote for the day
…faces are but a gallery of pictures, and talk but a tinkling cymbal, where there is no love.
Francis Bacon (1625) *Essays*, 'Of Friendship'

Faith links

Christian and Jewish
The kindness and understanding shown by Ruth and Boaz
Ruth: 1 and 2

Branching out

 Make a 'sound effects' tape of human voices, e.g. scream, laughter, yawning, etc.

 Add speech and thought bubbles to famous paintings, e.g. *The Scream* by Munch, *The Laughing Cavalier* by Hals, *Child with a Dove* by Picasso.

 Play 'Walk the walk' where pupils demonstrating different moods/emotions walk across the room and sit down on a chair.

Give us a clue

PREPARATION NEEDED

Three chairs

3 people to play Anger, Sadness and Fear

a set of speech bubbles saying: 'What's wrong', and the three rebuffs

a mac, hat, magnifying glass and notebook and pen.

a picture symbol for anger, sadness, and fear

WHAT TO DO

Leader steers events, holds up the speech bubbles as the words are spoken and the picture symbols as each case is solved.

This morning our assembly is about understanding other people. Watch carefully.

(First person scowls and angrily stomps across room with clenched fist. Then throws him/herself into a chair, arms folded, foot tapping.)
Leader: 'Hello (name).' **Anger:** 'Clear off!'

(Second person cries and with hands over face, and hunched body walks slowly to chair and sits down with face in hands and elbows resting on knees.)
Leader: 'Hello (name).' **Sadness:** 'Go away.'

(Third person rushes across the room, looking behind them, shoulders hunched and hands clasped, sits on edge of chair, he/she keeps looking over their shoulder wringing hands.)
Leader: 'Hello (name).' **Fear:** 'Leave me alone!'

Well really! I only said hello! The trouble is people don't always tell you when something is wrong. Sometimes they seem to be cross with us or are rude to us and we don't know why. I think that's what has happened here. People often try and hide their feelings. But if we look carefully we can often see for ourselves. It's a bit like being a detective. *(Hold up detective props.)* Have you seen detectives in films and on television? *(Look through magnifying glass.)* They are always looking for clues. We can do the same to find out what's wrong with our three friends here. Who wants to help solve the mystery and be a detective? *(Volunteer puts on detective clothes.)* Meet **Detective Inspector** (pupil's surname). Now **DI** (name), we need to look at three different sorts of

clues, faces, bodies and actions (the things people do). I'll make notes of any important information we find.

(Leader takes detective to Anger, encourage walking round and looking closely.) Have you noticed anything about his/her face? *(Note down what is discovered.)* What about his/her body language? *(Make note.)* And his/her actions, what is he/she doing? *(Make note.)* Now let's think about our clues. *(Read back notes.)* Mmm, tricky. Let's ask the audience to help us solve the mystery. Does anyone know what is wrong with this person? You think they're angry? **DI** (name) what do you think? Let's go and ask.
Leader: 'Excuse me, are you angry about something?' **Anger:** 'Yes I am!'
Leader: Well done everyone we have solved the case! *(Hold up symbol.)* *(Repeat procedure with new volunteers for detecting Sadness and Scared.)*

Of course we still don't know **why** these people are feeling angry, sad and scared. But at least we know that they are feeling that way. Instead of feeling cross with them, we can offer them our help. *(Approach each person.)*
Leader: 'Can I help you?' **Anger:** 'The other kids keep teasing me. It makes me really cross!' **Sadness:** 'No one will play with me. I'm so sad and lonely.' **Fear:** 'Someone is bullying me. I'm scared they're going to hurt me.'
Leader: 'Come on. Let's talk to (head/deputy) about it. He/she'll sort it out.'

Are you a good detective? Do you look at other people and look for clues? Knowing how people are feeling, helps us understand them. We might even be able to help them feel better.

Forgive and forget

Rub it out, don't rub it in

YOU WILL NEED

Flip chart, marker, pencil, eraser, pupils to mime Sam, Tim, Kim, Peter.

Begin by practising actions,* scowled, stamped his foot and clenched his fist.

(Write FORGIVE and FORGET at the head of two columns. Introduce characters.)
Meet Sam, Tim, Kim and Peter. Today we are going to hear the story of Sam who couldn't forgive and forget when someone upset him. *(Write 'forgive' on flip chart lightly, in pencil.)* To forgive and forget is like rubbing out a mistake so you can't see it anymore. *(Rub out wrong spelling.)* Sam didn't, he *scowled, stamped his foot and clenched his fists,* whenever Tim, Kim and Peter tried to speak to him.

On MONDAY Sam went out for a walk and fell into a deep hole. Tim came along and offered to help him out. But Sam * so Tim couldn't hold his hand to pull him out. 'You broke my ball,' Sam yelled. 'I said sorry,' said Tim. So Sam had to scramble out on his own and went home dirty and tired. On TUESDAY Sam went on a school trip without his lunch. Kim offered him a sandwich. But Sam*, so he couldn't hold the sandwich. 'You forgot my book,' yelled Sam. 'I said sorry,' said Kim. Sam got very hungry and went home miserable. On WEDNESDAY Sam went to the cinema on the bus, he lost his money. He met Peter who bought a ticket for him. But Sam*, so Peter couldn't give him the ticket. 'You trod on my foot,' yelled Sam. 'I said sorry,' said Peter. Sam walked away very cross and had to walk home.

The next day was Sam's birthday His classmates had planned a surprise. As Peter walked in they sang *Happy Birthday* and held out a present. Sam *, so he couldn't take his present. 'Last year you forgot my birthday,' he shouted. 'This is to show we are sorry,' said his friends. But Sam just could not forgive them and went away grumbling and wondering why he never had anyone to play with.

Why didn't Sam have anyone to play with? How did he feel? Who did Sam need to forgive? *(Write names on the list.)* What did he need to forget? *(List on chart.)* He needed to rub out all those things he remembered. Then he wouldn't feel like this *(all clench fists)* he'd feel... *(unclench and wave hands)*.

Prayers and Thinking

Ask pupils to shut eyes and clench fists. Think of someone you are angry with, or who is angry with you. Think about saying sorry or forgiving them. Listen to a line from the Lord's Prayer – 'Forgive us our sins, as we forgive those who sin against us'. Unclench fists and shake hands with the people sitting next to you.

Quote for the day

Whenever you're wrong admit it; whenever you're right, shut up.
Ogden Nash (1957) *A Word to Husbands*

Faith links

Christian
The Last Supper
Matthew 26: 17–30

Jewish
Yom Kippur

Muslim
Laila-ul-Barh

Branching out

 Using newspapers/ news clips, brainstorm (a) what has caused war and fighting in a current situation, national/local /international; (b) who do people need to say sorry to or forgive?

 Using a current/ personal/historical/ class/imaginary situation, write a poem: I am sorry ...I am sorry ...I am sorry ...Please forgive me (for thoughts/ words/actions)

 Play a game of 'Snap'. Each time a pair is laid, shout SORRY and to claim the cards, name a situation where someone might need to say sorry (e.g. said something hurtful, wouldn't play with someone, etc.)

I'm sorry! OK?

PREPARATION NEEDED

2 large flashcards
(1) SORRY
(2) FORGIVE
each with a face to
show the emotion,

a pupil with a
punctured ball or piece
of broken equipment,

a member of staff
primed to arrive late
with a pile of books,

two pupils primed to
have a chat, any other
relevant interruptions,

a story to begin to tell.

(Introduce a story you are going to read / tell / act. Begin the story.) Once upon a time.... *(A member of staff interrupts by arriving late for Assembly, walks across the room, carrying a pile of books and looking hassled. You look a little annoyed. He / she stops in a prominent place.)* I'm so SORRY I'm late, a cat walked into my classroom and I had to get it out. *(You smile.)* That's OK. I understand. We can't have cats coming to school! *(Wait for him / her to sit down.)*

(Begin the story again. A pupil interrupts, coming in looking very worried, carrying a piece of broken equipment relevant to you, the assembly leader eg. punctured ball – PE teacher / broken mug. You look more annoyed. Pupil stops holds up broken object and addresses you...) Sorry Mr___ / Ms ___, your I broke your _____ and was trying to fix it but I couldn't. *(You smile again)* That's OK...we'll see if we can mend it later. Thank you for owning up. Sit down and don't worry about it.

(Try to get the story started again. This time two pupils begin talking in the assembly). *(Very annoyed)* Come out here you two! *(Both come out; pupil 1 is holding his / her stomach and has a hand over their mouth.)* *(Pupil 2)* We're really SORRY but _____ is feeling sick and I asked if he / she wanted me to take them to the toilet.

(With some haste and concern for pupil 1, accept the apology) That's OK you'd best go quickly.

(Look at your watch) There's no time now to have the story, but let's think about what's happened this morning.

(Ask the pupils how they think you felt while you were trying to tell the story. They will probably reply 'angry, annoyed, cross' etc. Ask pupils to mime these.)

Is that how I felt all the time? *(Encourage pupils to think about when you smiled.)* What made me smile? (when each person said SORRY.) *(Pupil holds up SORRY flashcard and mimes SORRY face.)*

Can you remember what I said to each one – *('That's OK'.)* That means I've forgiven them and now they can have a fresh start. I won't be angry with them for those things again. It's all forgotten. It would be awful if they had to spend the rest of the day worried that I am still cross with them *(Pupil holds up FORGIVE flashcard and mimes a smile of forgiveness.)*

(Point to SORRY flashcard.) What did they say? *(School reply)* SORRY
(Point to FORGIVE flashcard.) What did I do? *(School reply)* FORGIVE

(Sum up.) It's important to say sorry and put things right as quickly as possible. It's important to forgive anyone who says sorry and give them a fresh start.)

All's fair...

Fair and square

YOU WILL NEED

A flip chart, pen and Blu-Tack

(Draw a square on a flip chart.) Do you know the name of this shape? (Begin to draw another, make one side longer creating an irregular shape.) Is this a square? So what is special about squares? Yes all their sides are the same length. They are equal.

Have you heard the saying 'fair and square'? (On a clean page draw another large square and divide it into four smaller ones.) These will help us think about what that means.

When we play a game how do we try to make it fair? (Write a list of pupils' suggestions at the side of the square. With prompts if necessary make sure the list encompasses the following headings. Write one in each square - 'clear rules', 'no cheating', 'equal chance', 'fair judge' or referee.)

Let's use these squares to help us play a game. (Cut out four more squares numbered 1–4 to correspond with the smaller squares on the flip chart.) We will need four players. (Give each player a square and put Blu-Tack on the squares on the flip chart.) I'm the referee. These are the rules. When I say go you have to run round the room then stick your square on the right number by the time I count to 10. If I get to 10 before you get back, you're out.

(Play the game as described.) Didn't they play well? Let's have another go. We'll need four more players. (Make sure these players will cope with you cheating! Tell the first player they have to get round before you count to 3. When the second player is running count to 10 really quickly. The third player should return to find their Blu-Tack has been removed. Prevent the fourth player from returning on time by getting in their way!)

(By now there will be protests from both players and audience! Look back at the four headings and decide with them what was unfair.) Okay. That wasn't fair and square was it? I didn't give them the same chance did I? I didn't treat them equally just like the four sides of a square. I'm sorry, you can have another go. I promise to be fair. (Repeat game.) Was that better? Was I fair that time? What about you? Are you always fair?

Prayers and Thinking

Buddha said that there are three things that cannot be hidden...

the sun

the moon

and the truth.

(Instant Assembly: Draw a sun, moon and a tick inside a heart.
Prepared Assembly: Make a cardboard cloud, and the same shapes as above. As you speak Buddha's words, make the objects appear from behind the cloud.)

Let us try to find the truth in our own hearts and look for that which is right.

Quote for the day

Injustice anywhere is a threat to justice everywhere.
Martin Luther King, Letter from Birmingham Jail, Alabama, 16 April 1963

Faith links

Christian
Solomon and the baby
1 Kings, 3: 16–28

Jewish
Alexander and Katzya, a story from the Talmud

Branching out

 Take characters from well-known stories or TV soaps and 'put them on trial.' Use an old fashioned set of scales to 'weigh up the evidence' for and against them.

 Make up a new playground or board game and decide on a set of rules that are fair.

 Investigate Fair Trade goods for sale in supermarkets. Why are they called Fair Trade?

The trial of Harry Achnid

PREPARATION NEEDED

A large hairy spider with long dangly legs and a friendly face. The spider should be attached to a length of elastic

a screen or cardboard box for 'the dock'

a table with a bible for the 'witness stand'

a tuffet of grass

a wig and gavel for the judge

WHAT TO DO

The narrator takes the part of the Judge

The following parts can also be played by the narrator by exchanging wigs and caps and holding up name cards as the different characters speak, or by pupils or other members of staff

Miss Muffet (with mob-cap, bowl and spoon)

Prosecution

Defence

Good morning everyone I want to introduce you to a very famous woman. This is Little Miss Muffet. You might have heard of her before. (*As you say the familiar nursery rhyme, Miss Muffet sits on tuffet and begins to eat, a spider descends at the side of her, Miss Muffet runs off screaming, spider remains.*) This is Harry Achnid, the spider in this famous tale. Harry is in court today. You are all members of the jury. You will decide if Harry is guilty or innocent. I am the judge. It is my job to see that Harry is treated fairly.

(*Put on wig and bang gavel.*) **Judge**: Silence in Court. Will the prisoner please stand. (*Spider placed dangling over dock.*) Harry Achnid you stand before this court accused of threatening behaviour towards Miss Muffet. How do you plead? **Defence:** Mr Achnid pleads not guilty my lord. **Judge:** Very well, we will hear the evidence against him first. Miss Muffet take the witness stand please. **Muffet:** I swear by almighty God that I will tell the truth, the whole truth and nothing but the truth.

Prosecution: Miss Muffet, please tell the court in your own words what happened. **Muffet:** Well sir, it was a lovely sunny day and I decided to take my lunch outside. I sat down on a tuffet... **Prosecution:** Exhibit A my lord. (*Shows jury.*) Please continue Miss Muffet. **Muffet:** I began to eat my lunch, sir. A lovely bowl of curds and whey, my favourite. **Prosecution:** Exhibit B my lord. (*Shows jury.*) **Muffet:** When this huge, ugly....**Defence:** Objection, my lord. **Judge:** Yes I agree, members of the jury you will ignore that last remark. Miss Muffet, please stick to the facts. This is not a beauty contest. It is a court of law! **Muffet:** As I was saying... this... this... spider leapt out from nowhere and waved his horrible hairy legs in my face. **Defence:** Objection, my lord. **Judge:** Yes I agree

the hairiness of Mr Achnid's legs is not on trial. Jury – ignore that remark. Continue. **Muffet:** So this...spider...this fly murdering monster...**Defence:** My Lord! **Judge:** Miss Muffet! I will not warn you again! **Muffet:** I'm sorry my lord. It's just that spiders are such horrible hairy things, spinning their sticky webs all over the place, running across the floor when you're trying to watch television, lurking in the bath tub...I know their sort, watching you with their evil eyes... just waiting to pounce. **Judge:** Silence! I think we have heard quite enough. Does the defence want to question the witness? **Defence:** Yes my lord.

Defence: Miss Muffet, you don't like spiders do you? **Muffet:** I don't know what you mean. **Defence:** Well, throughout your evidence today, we have heard nothing but a string of insults towards spiders. I put it to you that your story of threatening behaviour is nothing but a web of lies! There isn't one thread of evidence against poor Harry Achnid. I put it to you, Miss Muffet, that Mr Achnid did not threaten you at all. All he did was sit down beside you. In fact it was you that frightened him with all your screaming and shouting. **Muffet:** No! No! I tell you. He threatened me...the horrible eight legged beast...I had to run for my life!

Judge: Thank you Miss Muffet. Now you the jury must make up your mind. Did Harry Achnid really threaten Little Miss Muffet? Or did he merely sit next to her on the tuffet as she ate her curds and whey? Has Miss Muffet's prejudice and dislike of spiders got in the way of truth and fairness? Remember justice is about treating people fairly. You must now consider your verdict. Is Harry Achnid guilty or not guilty?

Hear, hear!

Hear no evil

YOU WILL NEED

Flipchart centre front, marker pen, 2 pupils, one with ruler pointing forward as volume indicator

WHAT TO DO

Write LISTEN at the top centre of the flipchart with an arrow pointing out from each end of the word to the edge of the paper. Over one arrow put a **+** over the other a **−**

What do we usually use for listening? (*Draw a large ear on each side of the flipchart.*) Listening is one of our senses. What are the others? (*Count off seeing, smelling, tasting, touching, listening, on fingers.*) We have five senses all with special jobs but quite often they help each other.

We listen to lots of things. There are things that are 'good to listen to', let's make them louder (*indicate the '+', one pupil behind the other moves him/her sideways in the direction of the +*) Some things are 'not good to listen to', it's good to turn them down so we can't hear (*indicate '−' volume indicator move sideways to −*)

Now, you tell me, what do we listen to? (*Take a suggestion.*) Is that 'good' or 'not good' listening? Why? So do we make it louder or softer? (*Pupils point or shout 'louder/quieter', indicators move..... write suggestion by ear on that side of the paper.*) (*Continue taking ideas eg lies, swearing, lessons, parents asking us to help, unkind names, people telling us to do wrong things, birds singing. Repeat the routine.*) Sometimes people speak to us without words. (*Beckon to a pupil to come out.*) What did I say to _____? Did he/she hear me? (*Wave to the assembly.*) What did I say? And you all heard because you waved back. What did you use to 'listen with?' (eyes) Just like when you use your ears, you could have ignored me, but it would have been a bit rude.

(*Sum up.*) We can choose what we listen to. What sort of people will we be if we listen to the 'not good' things (*Read list on − side of paper; encourage ideas of someone other people will not want to be friends with/cannot trust, get into trouble.*) What about if we listen to good things? (*Read list on + side; people will want to know us, trust us, be friends and talk to us.*) Let's make these things louder (*send indicators to + side pupils point*) and (*hand to ear, pupils copy*) do some really good listening.

Prayers and Thinking

Listen and think very carefully. I will whisper to you then you whisper it to someone near you. If you want to pray say it quietly to God first… 'I will try to listen to good things'. (If this is likely to cause a kerfuffle pupils can just whisper it to themselves.)

Quote for the day

Bore, n–A person who talks when you wish him to listen.
Ambrose Bierce (1842-1914) *The Devil's Dictionary*

Faith links

Christian and Jewish
Samuel in the Temple
1 Samuel 3

Moslem
Lailat-ul-Qadr

Branching out

 Listen to two short contrasting pieces of music. Talk about what was different.

 Play charades miming a phrase or feeling. Discuss how they worked out what was being 'said'.

 In pairs face to face, one pupil with ear muffs tries to work out what their partner is saying.

All ears!

PREPARATION NEEDED

Flip chart with outline of face with large ears

3 pupils each with a pair of large card ears (A, B and C with safety pins round edge of ears)

1 pupil (D) with a number of smaller card ears pinned all over him/her.)

WHAT TO DO

Group prepared to mime a scene to include, a pupil responding to a friend who is looking sad; waving hello/goodbye; beckoning; getting excited eg at a football match etc (see text)

(Leader) Can anyone guess what we are talking about this morning? *(Point to the flipchart.)* *(As pupils respond – repeat back 'Listening' and write on the flipchart. Pupil D comes in.)* Did you say listening? I'm all ears. I'll listen for you. *(Leader)* All ears!! That's a funny thing to say. What on earth does that mean? *(Pupils respond. Explain the phrase.)* OK _____ (pupil D) you go and listen. *(Pupil D quietly wanders around assembly room listening.)*

We do say some funny things about listening, lets look at some others. *(Pupil A comes in holding out an ear to you.)* *(Leader)* I don't want it. What are you doing? *(Pupil A)* Giving ear to what you say. *(Leader repeat as for pupil D. Pupil A wanders round offering his ears.)*

(Pupil B crawls in with his head to the ground.) What on earth are you doing? *(Pupil B)* Dad told me to keep my ear to the ground to find out if there are any football tickets left. *(Repeat as for D. Pupil B crawls around.)*

(Pupil C walks in holding the ears to the side of his head so the pins can be seen) _____ (pupil C) aren't your ears sore with all those pins? Why have you got that many? *(Pupil C)* I wasn't listening this morning so my teacher said I should pin my ears back and listen. *(Leader repeat as for previous pupils. Pupil C walks around 'listening'.)*

(Leader) While they're listening let's watch a mime *(Pupils A,B,C,D freeze where they are busy 'listening' but not watching.)* *(Pupils mime to communicate, clearly, situations and how they respond to them.)*

(Leader ask assembly what was 'said' in the mime. Point out that no words were used but that lots of things were 'said' in other ways.) *(Work through the mime asking.)* What did _____ 'say'? How did they 'say 'it? How did you know? (Expressions/ body language/ signs etc) *(Assembly to copy.)*

(After each one, ask pupils A,B,C,D.) Were you listening to what they said? *(Each replies.)* No, I was busy.... keeping my ear to the ground/ pinning my ears back/ giving ear to/ all ears.

(Sum up) A, B, C, D used only their ears to listen. What did the rest of us use? *(all point to eyes.)* We used our eyes to see how someone was behaving, what they were doing, what they were 'saying' *(Draw eyes on face on flipchart.)*

(Draw a heart under the face, all draw hearts in the air.) We also used our heart to listen to how someone was feeling. We don't always use words to say things, so to really listen we need to use our eyes and hearts too.

Only the loving find love

The castle walls

Prayers and Thinking

A large sheet of paper, a marker pen, scissors

(Draw a large heart and call it 'Love'. Give this to a pupil at one side of the room. Another pupil at the other side should represent King Nolove.)

King Nolove lives alone in a castle with high walls and never lets anyone in.

(Stand a group of children between the king and 'Love' to represent the walls.)

'Love' knocked on the walls of the castle, calling out the king's name and trying to get close to him.

King Nolove sent Love away and built his walls higher and thicker. *(Add more children.)*

(The scene should be repeated several times, adding more children to form the wall.)

The walls became so deep that no one could get in **(ask others to try) but** King Nolove couldn't get out either when he tried.

The king got very lonely and was sorry that he had sent 'Love' away. He knew he wanted love but couldn't reach it.

(Ask the children what he should do. Use their ideas to act out an escape/rescue, e.g. children come out and help him take down the walls so that he can reach 'love'.)

When the king finally reached 'Love', **(is given the heart)** he shared it with the all the others who helped him and was never lonely again. **(King passes the heart around for everyone to hold.)**

(Draw a love heart with a ribbon around it on a flip chart.)

Love is a very special present that we can give to others. Think about someone you care about. It might be someone in your family or a friend. Imagine their name or face drawn on the love heart. Close your eyes and try to see a picture of yourself giving them the love heart and them giving you a love heart back.

Quote for the day
... only the loving find love, and they never have to seek for it.
DH Lawrence (1885-1930) *Search for Love*

Faith links

Christian
Description of love 1 Corinthians: 13, 4-7
Buddhist
Symbolism of lotus flower to represent Lord Buddha and his teachings

Branching out

 Make up a 'traditional' song and ring dance to the tune of *Old Roger*. You could start with 'There once was a king who just could not find love...'

 Construct a tall ladder to scale King Nolove's walls from rolled up newspapers. Stick a word or a symbol on each rung saying how we can show others that we care.

 Make a graffiti wall from paper bricks. Write words and phrases about the things that get in love's way on the wall.

King Nolove's garden

PREPARATION NEEDED

A set of red paper hearts

a paper crown

a paper rose

a large key

paper money or gold coins

an advert for love (see story)

WHAT TO DO

Presenter reads the story

Volunteers to play King Nolove and his subjects

Words in bold should be acted out by the presenter and the volunteers

There was once a king who lived in a palace *(choose someone and place a crown on their head)* with a beautiful rose garden. **(King smells paper rose.)** All around his garden was a high wall. The gates were closed to keep other people out. **(King locks gate with large key.)** The king enjoyed his roses and his palace but he was lonely. His name was King Nolove.

One day the king realised that what was missing in his life was love. **(Presenter holds up a heart.)** He decided to go out and look for some. He went outside his walls, locking his gates. He travelled North, South, East and West **(King walks around the room searching)** looking high and low and far and wide. He told everyone he met 'I'm looking for love, have you seen any?' The people laughed, 'Don't you know you can't just go out and find love?' they said. Eventually a very tired King Nolove went back to his palace and locked his gates behind him.

King Nolove decided that if he couldn't just find love, he would have to go out and buy some. He went outside. **(King locks gates.)** He took plenty of money with him and gave it away to all the people he met outside. **(King hands out money to audience.)** 'I need some love,' he said, 'How much does it cost?' The people took his money because they were poor, but they all laughed at him and thought him a fool. 'Don't you know money can't buy love,' they said. Sadly the king went back to his palace. **(King locks gates.)**

King Nolove worried that he might never have love, so he wrote out an advert for THE KING'S PERFECT LOVE, and put it in the paper. The advert listed all the things he wanted. **(King pretends to write advert.)** 'My love should like roses, gardening, beautiful things, polishing jewels, bananas in custard, *Match of the Day*' ...The list went on and on for two whole pages! It was in the paper for weeks but no one wrote back. The king rang up the paper and complained. 'No one has applied for the job as my perfect love!' 'Of course not,' said the editor, 'Don't you know that there is no such thing as a perfect love?' The king slammed down the phone and rushed into his rose garden to calm down.

As he walked, **(King smells roses.)** he could hear people on the other side of the wall. 'The King's roses smell nice; I wish we could see them.' 'No chance of that, he never lets anyone in. His gates are always shut.' 'What a shame. No wonder he's so lonely.' King Nolove suddenly knew what to do. He rushed across and unlocked his gates. 'Come in!' he shouted. 'The roses are so beautiful, come and share them.' Astonished people soon filled the garden.

From then on the gates were always open. **(King throws away key.)** The king held parties. Children played on the lawns. As the king opened his gates he opened his heart and began to give love to others. **(King gives out red hearts to audience.)** And others gave their love to him. **(Presenter gives heart to king.)** 'Now at last I know what others know,' he said. Love cannot be found, or bought. There is no ideal or perfect love. 'Love comes from loving others.' And from that very day he was no longer called King Nolove, he changed his name by deed poll to King Truelove! **(King holds up heart.)**

Yours respectfully

Planet status

This is 'Posher'. **(Draw small star top left of flip chart.)** This is 'Lowly'. **(Draw crescent moon top right.)** The 'Poshuns' **(point to 3 pupils)** built a tall rocket. **(Draw at side of star & mime.)** The 'Lowlies' **(other pupils)** built a flying saucer. **(Draw and mime.)** They each set off to live on a new planet **(draw large 'Saturn - like' planet in the middle)** called 'Status'. **(Write 'Status' above centre ring.)** The Poshuns went first, 5, 4,3,2,1. Lift off! Whoosh! They landed at the top. **(Draw arrow showing journey and rocket at top.)** The 'Lowlies' went next, 5, 4, 3, 2, 1. Lift off! Wurble, wurble! They landed at the bottom. **(Draw arrow and saucer at bottom.)** The 'Poshuns' built tall towers. **(Mime and draw.)** The 'Lowlies' dug homes underground. **(Mime and draw.)** The 'Poshuns' worked on the internet. The 'Lowlies' grew fruit on their 'Poorlygon' trees.

When the 'Poshuns' went walking they held their heads high and their noses in the air. **(Mime.)** When the 'Lowlies' walked they stooped with their heads down and their eyes to the ground. **(Mime.)** Look what happened when they went walking at the same time! **(Bump into each other.)** When this happened, the 'Poshuns' pushed the 'Lowlies' to their knees who hid their faces in the mud. **(Mime.)** But one day something happened to change this. A nasty bug arrived. **(Draw flying bug over planet.)** Bzzzz the bug flew all over Planet Status, spreading its nasty germs everywhere. One by one the 'Poshuns' got poorly and went to bed **(Chairs end to end.)** But the 'Lowlies' stayed well by eating the fruit of the 'Poorlygon' tree.

Knowing that the 'Poshuns' might die, the 'Lowlies' took some of the Poorlygon fruit and shared it with them. **(Mime.)** As they bent over the beds and the 'Poshuns' took the fruit, they looked each other in the eyes for the first time. And from that moment on, something else grew on Planet Status as well as 'Poorlygon' Trees. RESPECT!

(Write word on planet.)
Where do you think the respect grew?

Prayers and Thinking

You will need a coin, flip chart and pen

(Spin coin.) Every coin has two sides – heads and tails. **(Draw.)** Together both sides are worth something. On its own, each side is worth nothing. Respect is like this. It has two sides – You – and me. **(Write each word inside its own circle.)** Both sides need to learn to respect each other, **(draw two way arrows)** only then do we have something really valuable.

Quote for the day

The worst sin towards our fellow creatures is not to hate them, but to be indifferent to them: that's the essence of inhumanity.
George Bernard Shaw (1897) *The Devil's Disciple*

Faith links

Christian
Respect should not depend on appearance or wealth
James 2: 1–7

Jewish
The treatment of the Jewish people by the Nazis

Branching out

 Talk about the holy books of different world faiths. How do the different religions show their respect for these? What do these signs of respect have in common?

 Rolling out a red carpet is a traditional sign of respect – make a collage which incorporates images of people worthy of such respect – are they always famous? What does status mean?

 Work out some further role play for Planet Status – before and after the nasty bug. Why were the characters called the 'Poshuns' and the 'Lowlies'?

Rapping respect

PREPARATION NEEDED

The seven letters of the word RESPECT, each one on a separate card

drum machine (optional)

at least 7 pupils with time to practise the rap and the turning over of the cards!

WHAT TO DO

This rap can be performed by a group of pupils

or

said by the assembly leader

(Pupils stand in line to spell the word respect with letter cards initially turned away.) See if you can guess what our assembly is about today. *(Turn letters one at a time.)* What does the word mean? Do you think respect is important? Why? We think respect is so important we want to teach you how to spell it. Name the letters with me? *(Point to each one in turn.)* Let's play a memory game to help you learn it. Who wants a go? *(Audience members take it in turn to close their eyes while a letter is turned round – then open their eyes and say which letter is missing.)* Ok now you know how to spell RESPECT. Can you say it in the same rhythm as me? *(As you say the rhythm, the cards are turned to face the audience.)* RES-PE-CT. Say 'RESPECT for you' 'RESPECT for me.' Say it in the same rhythm. Now you know the chorus of 'Rapping Respect.' Join in when we get to that bit. Are you ready to rap? Let's go!

(Chorus) RES-PE-CT
Respect for you / Respect for me

All the world's people
Heads high not bowed,
Feelin' good
And feelin' proud.
(Repeat Chorus.)

Away with prejudice,
Fear and strife.
Y'all gotta show
Respect in your life.
(Repeat Chorus.)

A little respect
Is the only way,
Show some understanding
In the livelong day.
(Repeat Chorus.)

Do unto others
A wise man said,
Carry that message
In your head.
(Repeat Chorus.)

Make sure this message
Is one that's heard.
Respect is a very
Important word!
(Repeat Chorus.)

Why do you think respect is such an important word? Who was the wise man in the rap? What did he say?

What happens when people don't respect each other? Let's do the rap again. Listen carefully to the words.

We will remember them

Eleven is special number

YOU WILL NEED

A flip chart and pen

Eleven is a special number. (*Write it down and count to eleven using your fingers.*) Were there enough? (*Try again – with help – and use your head for number 11. Explain your head helps you remember things.*) Remembering can be hard, sometimes we forget things. Our assembly is about remembering and trying not to forget.

(*Write down the date 11–11– and the current year.*) Who can remember what this means? It is a very special date.

(*Draw a large clock face and – with help – number it. Leave space around it for further words. Draw on the hands to indicate 11 o'clock.*) Can anyone remember what time this is? It is a very special time.

(*Explain that at 11 o'clock, on 11th November people try to remember soldiers who went to war and died.*) They remember them because they gave up their lives for other people. People try not to forget the soldiers and that war is a terrible thing. This special day is called Remembrance Day.

(*Write 'Remembrance' above the clock.*) Remembrance means to remember. (*Count the letters in the word.*)

Eleven is a special number, it reminds us to stop at 11 o'clock on Remembrance Day and stand in silence to show we haven't forgotten the people who died. We can wear a poppy to help us remember too. (*Draw a poppy in the centre of the clock.*)

(*If time, 11 words about war can be written around the clock and used as a basis for a simple prayer/reflection.*)

Prayers and Thinking

(*Listen to these words and some music from the Remembrance Day Service.*)

'They shall not grow old as we that are left grow old:

Age shall not weary them, nor the years condemn.

At the going down of the sun and in the morning

We will remember them.

We will remember them.'

(**Play The Last Post** (optional).)

Quote for the day

If ye break faith with us who die,
We shall not sleep,
though poppies grow
In Flanders fields.

John MacCrae (1872–1918) In *Flanders Fields*

Faith links

Christian
Jesus is crucified
Matthew 27: 27–54

Muslim
Eid al-Adha
(Festival of Sacrifice)

Branching out

 Pupils can carry out their own extended role plays, similar to the assembly overleaf. They could then role play a Remembrance Day parade and the laying of poppy wreaths.

 Each pupil can make a poppy and bring it to assembly. Poppies can be laid at the front or collected as pupils leave. The poppies could include a personal thought for Remembrance Day.

 Pupils can make their own clock face and calendar page for Remembrance Day which includes their own words or those from MacCrae's poem or the Remembrance Day service.

It'll be over by Christmas

PREPARATION NEEDED

Photographs of soldiers from the First World War, the trenches and the battlefields

happy, proud, scared feelings symbols/ photos

a selection of Remembrance Day poppies

a collection tin and some money

a set of small white crosses

music — *The Last Post* for prayers and thinking

music — *It's a Long Way to Tipperary*

WHAT TO DO

The adult presenter acts as a narrator and leader of the role play.

You will need to select a group of pupils to act as soldiers.

(Adult acts as narrator, holds up the photographs of soldiers.) The First World War began in the summer of 1914. People said it was the war to end all wars. Thousands of young men joined the army to fight for their country and to march off to war. *(Select a group of pupils to represent soldiers, practise standing to attention and marching.)*

(Soldiers introduce themselves to the audience, saying their names and rank.) We are so proud to be part of this war and to fight for our country. *(Hold up feeling symbols/ photographs for happy and proud. Walk amongst the soldiers, shaking their hands.)* Good luck lads, we'll be back by Christmas.

(Line up the soldiers behind you in front of the audience.) We all got ready to go. A huge crowd gathered to cheer us on our way! *(Wave to the audience and encourage them to play the part of the crowd and to wave and cheer.)*

(March around the room singing to It's a Long Way to Tipperary. Encourage the audience to join in and to clap in time to the march. Then return to the front and stand quietly.)

But when we got to Flanders, it wasn't anything like we thought it was going to be. *(Hold up photographs of the trenches, guns etc.)* There were machine guns, tanks, flame throwers, gas, bombs… We were so scared. *(Hold up feelings symbol/photo.)* There was no glory in that. Most of us didn't make it. And they were wrong; the war wasn't over by Christmas. It lasted for four whole years.

One by one we died. Over 14 million people died altogether. *(Hand out white crosses to each soldier and ask him or her to stand with their heads bowed.)*

In the fields where the fighting took place and the soldiers died, red poppies started to flower. *(Hand each soldier a red poppy to hold with their cross.)* One of the soldiers, Colonel John MacCrae wrote a poem about the poppies:

In Flanders' Fields the poppies blow
Beneath the crosses, row on row,

On Remembrance Day people think about those who have died or been injured through war. We remember them and thank them for giving up their lives for others. We hope that no more people will have to die and that the world can live in peace.

People buy poppies to show they remember. The money from the poppies helps people who have been hurt through war.

(Give some money to some of the audience to bring to the front and put in a collection box and present them with poppies to wear.)

Trust you!

Don't let me down

(Ask for a volunteer and stand him/her on chair, holding their hand.) This is Sam the Sky-Diver. What do you think he enjoys doing at weekends? *(Indicate flip chart.)* *(Encourage 'Sam' to jump off the chair a couple of times.)* When Sam jumps off the chair he/she trusts me. *(Write 'trust' above the parachute.)* What does he/she trust me to do? (Make sure he/she doesn't fall.) How do I do that? (Hold hand) *(Thank Sam, return to seat.)*

When Sam jumps from an aeroplane he loves falling fast through the air but he always has one of these strapped to his back. *(Indicate parachute.)* What is it? *(Write on canopy.)* Sam trusts his parachute. What does he trust it to do?

(Open, stop him crashing, etc.) We might not go sky-diving but everyday we trust other people to do things for us. Can you think of someone you trust? *(Write on canopy.)* What do we trust them to do? *(Continue with more suggestions, e.g. parent/carer to wake you up at the right time; dentist to treat the right tooth; friend to keep a secret; hairdresser not to cut off all your hair; God; bus-driver; teacher; car-drivers.)*

We trust lots of people everyday. *(Call out Sam, stand on chair again, give him carrier bag.)* Would Sam jump out of the plane and trust a plastic bag to keep him safe? *(Sam jump from chair holding bag above head.)* No, that would be silly. Would you let me pull out your tooth?... Your friend choose some medicine for you? No that would be silly too. Sam trusts his parachute because he knows it is safe. And it's good there are other people we can trust who are safe. (Recap from canopy and any others they want to mention.)

Prayers and Thinking

(Call out a confident pupil – cover their eyes with your hands) _____ can't see what's happening. He/she is having to trust me. Sometimes we can't see what might happen and feel afraid. We need someone we can trust. Some of you trust that God is always with you. Cover your eyes, think of someone you can trust... now say thank you for that person.

Quote for the day

Never trust the man who hath reason to suspect that you know he hath injured you.
Henry Fielding (1707–1754) *Jonathan Wild*

Faith links

Christian
The miraculous catch of fish
John 21

Jewish
The Exodus

Branching out

 Blindfold a pupil who is willing to trust someone to lead them round the room. Ask them what it felt like.

 Make a list of people we trust and discuss how we trust them (doctor, teacher, friend, etc).

 Put 'POST Its' around classroom on things we trust. (heating, lighting, ceiling won't fall down, etc).

PREPARATION NEEDED

Loose change

flip chart

marker pen

pupils to be Joe and Jim

a jacket for Jim

I'm banking on you

I need two people I can trust. (**Write TRUST on flip chart.**) What does trust mean? (**Write suggestions under TRUST.**) I need someone I can trust to look after my money. (**Choose two volunteers, give them some coins each.**) Now you won't lose it will you? You won't give it to anyone else? (**Send them back to their seats.**)

(**Give Joe some coins – Tell story.**) This is Joe. Joe was going on holiday. He had just been paid but didn't want to take a lot of money with him. 'I'll ask Jim to put it in the bank, he's a good mate I can trust him,' thought Joe. (**Calls Jim, gives him the money.**) 'I'll do it tomorrow,' said Jim. (**Just to make sure, Joe asks assembly to put their hands up if Jim does anything else with the money.**) So, Joe set off for the airport. Jim put the money in his pocket and walked home. On the way he heard the ice cream van. 'Cor I could murder a 99,' (**or popular ice cream**) thought Jim, 'I'll borrow some of Joe's money 'til I get home.'

(**Pupils' hands up.**) Is something wrong?... What's the matter? (Not his money – Joe trusts him, etc) Was Joe right to trust him?

As Jim turned into the High Street he saw the Arcade. He liked playing on the race track machine. He put his hand in his pocket and took out 50p from Joe's money. It was so exciting he had another go... and another.

(**Pupils' hands up.**) Now what's he done wrong?... Why is that wrong? Was Joe right to trust him?

Jim was there nearly an hour! I must

stop and go home,' he said. 'It's getting dark.'

Outside the Arcade was a lady with a tin; she was collecting for the homeless people. 'Joe would give her some money,' thought Jim, and put 20p in the box.

(**Pupils hands up.**) He's not at it again is he?... What's he done this time? (**Don't get caught up in moral issues other than it's not his money to give.**) Was Joe right to trust him?

The next morning Jim got up. He put on his coat to go to the Bank and put his hand in the pocket. Where was Joe's money? Jim thought of the money he had spent yesterday and realised Joe's money was all gone. 'Oh no!' said Jim, 'I haven't got that much money to pay him back.' (**Ask what Jim could do to pay back the money.**) Joe did lots of jobs to earn the money. He vacuumed the floor, (**get pupils to vacuum with Jim**) cleaned the car, (**action**) dug the garden (**action**) and did the washing up (**action**). When Joe got home his money still wasn't in the bank. 'Where is it'? asked Joe, 'I thought I could trust you.' Jim said sorry and promised to pay it all back.

What do you think Joe will do with his money next time?... Why? (Can't trust Jim.) (**Draw a sad face under TRUST labelled Jim.**)

(**Ask two pupils for your money back.**) Can I trust them?... Why? (**Draw 2 happy faces with pupils names.**) It's good to be able to trust people.

Wise guys and gals

Solomon's solution

YOU WILL NEED

Flip chart, marker pen, scissor

WHAT TO DO

Get characters to mime as you tell the story. When the pupils say 'a great King' they raise arms and bend elbows as a strong man. For 'a wise King' they tap forehead with forefinger

Write GREAT on the flip chart in large letters. Ask assembly who they think is a great person and discuss why. If necessary prompt with, footballer, pop singer, film star, etc.

(Tell story.) King Solomon was a great King. *(Do action. Cut circular badge and write A GREAT KING, give it to pupil willing to be Solomon. Ask 'what was Solomon?')* He made sensible laws and everyone trusted him. *(Point to Solomon's badge and ask.)* What sort of King was Solomon? *(All reply.)* One day two women were having an argument *(choose 2 pupils).* They were arguing over a baby! *(Pupil stand in middle and suck thumb.)* 'That's my baby,' said one. 'No, it's mine,' shouted the other. *(Repeat to continue argument, encouraging two sides of assembly to join in.)* 'I know,' said the woman, 'let's ask the king.' And off they went.

Now Solomon was...? *(point to badge)* but he was great because he was wise. *(Do action, cut 2nd badge and write A WISE KING. Ask 'what sort of King is Solomon?' Pupils repeat both badges with actions.)* He thought and he thought. Suddenly he had an idea! 'I'll cut the baby in two and you can have half each,' he said. 'What a brilliant idea,' said one woman. *(Solomon lifts arms to cut baby.)* No! shouted the other, 'Don't hurt him/her. Let her have him/her.' 'Now I know who is the real mother,' said Solomon.

(Ask pupils which one they think is the mother and why. How did Solomon find out?) That was a wise and sensible decision. Solomon wasn't a famous footballer or pop singer or film star, he was...? *(Point to 1st badge)* because he was...? *(Point to 2nd badge)*

Prayers and Thinking

A wise old owl sat in his tree. He looked to see what he could see. *(Draw 2 eyes.)* He learned from what he saw and heard. *(Draw 2 ears.)* Let's all be like that wise old bird. Lord help us to look and listen so we can make wise decisions.

Quote of the day

When pride comes, then comes disgrace, but with humility comes wisdom. *The Bible*

Faith links

Christian
Jesus rides into Jerusalem – Palm Sunday
Matthew 21: 1–11

Jewish
The anointing of King David

Buddhist
Story of Siddhartha Gantama – Wesak

Branching out

 Find people who had the title 'Great', e.g. Alexander, Herod. Did they deserve it?

 Look at a local/county map. Make a list of place names beginning with Great.

 Make a set of situation cards, e.g. break a window, lose a library book, tear new coat. In two teams think of a wise and unwise solution, e.g. tell mum/swap coats with someone else.

A great climb down

PREPARATION NEEDED

A slightly large crown,

royal robes

sword,

fancy slippers

'Esmerelda and Prime Minister who will act as the story is told

'horse' with reins

Old lady on chair at front

young man in a doorway

little girl in the crowd

Esmerelda had just become queen. **(Esmerelda walking up and down, in jeans and T shirt, looking quite important.) (Prime Minister addresses assembly.)** 'When I clap my hands, please bow to your queen and say, Your Majesty' **(Claps hands.)** 'Come on, I must go into town and meet my people,' Esmerelda said to the Prime Minister, 'They will want to know who I am and that I am going to be a great Queen for them.' 'Your Majesty,' gasped the Prime Minister, 'you can't go like that! What will they think! You must put on your Royal robes and silk slippers and golden crown. Your people will want to see that you are a powerful and important queen who will look after them.' Esmerelda shrugged, she hadn't been a queen before, the Prime Minister must know what he is talking about.

The Prime Minister called for the Royal robes **(Pupil brings in robes and puts them on Esmerelda.) (PM claps hands.)** 'These are so heavy and I trip over them,' complained Esmerelda. 'But you look like a great queen,' said the PM 'Bring the queen's crown.' **(Crown put on Esmerelda's head. It keeps slipping over her eyes.) (PM claps hands.)** 'Now I can't see my people,' said Esmerelda. 'Never mind, they can see that you are a great queen. Bring the silk slippers,' called the PM. **(Slippers put on her feet.) (PM claps hands.)** 'But it looks like rain. My feet will get soaked,' groaned Esmerelda 'Of course they won't,' laughed the PM, 'you will be riding on the Royal horse.' Esmerelda was lifted onto the Royal horse. **(Stand behind and hold reins of 'horse'.) (PM claps hands) (PM hands Esmerelda a sword.)** 'There now you are a queen.'

The Prime Minister led the horse out of the palace into the town. **(PM leads 'horse' round the assembly.)**
All the people cheered and shouted **(Encourage assembly to cheer.)** As they

passed the Town Hall Esmerelda saw an old lady reaching out to shake her hand. Esmerelda reached out too, but she couldn't reach she was too high up. The old lady was so disappointed. Further along the road, they passed a young man in a shop doorway, he was shivering as he waved. Esmerelda tried to wave but the Royal robes got in the way. A little girl called out, **(from assembly)** but Esmerelda couldn't see her as the crown had fallen over her eyes. 'Stop!' yelled Esmerelda, 'This is hopeless. This isn't being a great queen.' She handed the sword and the crown to the PM, climbed down off the horse, took off the royal robes and set off, back up the road.

The Prime Minister shouted and clapped his hands **(PM claps hands – assembly responds.)** 'Come back, you are the Queen.' 'And that's exactly what I am going to be', called Esmerelda as she got to the shop doorway. 'Here take these to keep you warm', she said as she gave the young man the Royal robes. She turned and walked into the crowds to find the little girl who had called her. She was thrilled to speak to the new Queen. The PM was still running behind clapping his hands to get the queen's attention. **(PM claps hands.)** It began to rain and Esmerelda's feet were getting wet but she didn't care. She set off for the Town Hall. Fortunately the old lady was still there. Esmerelda went over and gave her a hug. 'That's just what we need,' said the old lady 'a real queen, not someone who looks like one. She's going to be great!' **(PM claps hands.)**

(Put royal clothes back on. Ask.) Did Esmerelda need robes to be a great queen **or** was she great without? **(Remove robes.)** Why does the old lady think Esmerelda is going to be a great queen?

Word wars

Thumbs up, thumbs down

YOU WILL NEED

Flip chart and 2 marker pens (OPTIONAL – a personal memory where someone was unkind)

SUGGESTED MIMES

pulling faces behind someone's back, helping someone across the road, picking up someone who has fallen over, hiding someone's PE kit, sharing sweets, gossiping.

(Write the words KIND, with a thumbs up and UNKIND, with a thumbs down, at the top of the flip chart, use these hand signs throughout for the two words.) What does <u>kind</u> and <u>unkind</u> mean? What does a <u>kind</u> face look like? What does an <u>unkind</u> face look like? **(Pupils to mime.)**

We are going to play a thinking game. **(Divide assembly into 2 teams.)** I am going to call out a pupil from each team… I will whisper something to the pupil from team 1 to mime … For 2 points, the pupil from team 2 has to think, (a) what was mimed (b) what might have been said… For a bonus point the whole team has to decide if it is a KIND mime **(thumb up)** or UNKIND **(thumb down)** and put a either a tick in the KIND column or a cross in the UNKIND column. **(Use different colour markers.)**

(Start to play … after the mime ask)
1. Why was it kind/unkind?…
2. How would people feel when these things happen to them?
(Continue taking turns with the teams using different pupils each time and keeping the score. Add up points. Praise everyone for thinking hard about the mimes. Review which mimes got thumbs up/down.)

Who can remember someone being <u>unkind</u> to them? Who can remember someone being <u>kind</u>?… What did it feel like?… Which was best?… **(Share a memory of your own.)** Unkind words/ actions can hurt more than physical blows so let's stop and think before being <u>unkind</u> to someone and change to being kind instead.

Prayers and Thinking

(Optional – give 3 or 4 pupils a stone to drop into a bowl of water.)
Turn your thumbs down and think about a time you were unkind to someone. Think, 'Do I still need to say sorry?' (as you hear the stones drop in the water) make up your mind to do it. Some of you will believe that it hurts God when we are unkind and will want to say sorry to Him too… Now thumbs up and remember when someone was kind to you.

Quote of the day
Reckless words pierce like the sword, but the tongue of the wise brings healing
The Bible

Faith links

Christian
Stephen, first Christian martyr
Acts 6 and 7

Hindu
Ahimsa

Branching out

 Brainstorm kind and unkind words/ phrases. Use to write a kind/unkind poem.

 Mime a word to a partner using action and expression. Partner to guess if it is a kind or unkind word/what the word is.

 Watch a video cartoon and decide if we laugh at the kind or unkind things.

PREPARATION NEEDED

A 'victim', wearing a non-school jumper or some other unsuitable garment, with a name pinned to their front

a 'buddy' with a label pinned to his/her front

head teacher (or pupil dressed up)

5 bullies to the side with a sheet of scrap paper each

5 supporters in their seats

Stick and stones

LEADER: (*Introduce the victim.*) Meet —— —— (*Looking lonely, head down. Not the name of a pupil in the school.*) His/her dad had got a new job, but it meant the family had to leave their house and move to a new one a long way away. —— was finding it very hard. He/she didn't have any friends yet and even worse it was the first day of term and dad hadn't got his/her new school (jumper) yet. —— didn't know anyone in his/her new school and was feeling very shy and lonely.

HEAD: Hello —— welcome to …School. It's good to have you…etc. (*Call 'buddy' out and introduce him/her.*) This is … he/she will look after you and show you what to do until you are settled in. (*Turns to assembly.*) I want you to keep a look out too. If anyone is unkind, you are to wave your hand. (*Head walks off.*)

BUDDY: Come and meet some of the others. (*Leads —— round the room introducing staff and pupils. As they return to the front, one of the bullies strolls up, screws up the piece of paper, throws it like a stone making an unkind comment about the (jumper). —— hangs his/her head. Each of the bullies follow, throwing a 'stone' and making unkind comments. As each stone is thrown —— crumples a little more until he/she is crouched on the floor surrounded by the group. If pupils wave, stop and check what they saw happen. 'Buddy' is helpless against a group of 5.*)

BUDDY: I need some help. (*As supporters help, the bullies back off one by one.*)

SUPPORT 1: (*Comes from his/her seat to the front.*) Hey —— will you play with us at breaktime? (*Takes —— hand and lifts his/her arm.*)

SUPPORT 2: I hear you're good at maths will you help me with my homework? (*Comes out and lifts other arm.*)

SUPPORTs 3–5: (*Come out each making a positive comment and support ——, under the arms and round the waist. Together they all lift him/her into a standing position with his/her head still down.*)

BUDDY: (*Lifts up —— head.*) Let's go and show you our classroom. (*All leave together, —— in the middle.*)

LEADER: That was a dreadful thing to happen on ——'s first day. (*Calls —— over.*) Did that hurt? (—— *nods.*)

LEADER: I can't see any cuts or bruises where did it hurt?

VICTIM: Inside.

LEADER: Is it better now? (—— *nods again.*) What made it better?

VICTIM: When the others helped me and I knew I had some friends.

LEADER: (*Praise pupils for seeing the unkind things and recap them.*) There's a saying 'Sticks and stones can break our bones but names can never hurt us'. That doesn't always <u>feel</u> true. Saying unkind things does hurt, but 'kind words and a friend can help us mend.' Just as —— found out.

Community

Count me in

The buzz of belonging!

YOU WILL NEED

Flip chart, marker pens,
(OPTIONAL secretary/
caretaker/cleaner/cook
primed to be collected
and included in assembly)

I'm going to give you a clue to what today's assembly is about. If you guess it don't call out, wait until the end.
The word has three syllables; the first … (*flap your arms and buzz… bee*) the second … (*stretch your arms out wide… long*) the last… (*write ing on the flip chart*).

Now, to help us work it out, I need the youngest person here. (*Youngest pupil comes to stand at the front. Continue to ask for… and if necessary send pupil to collect … eldest pupil, eldest person, someone from yr. —, a member of the football club/team, an instrumentalist in the orchestra, secretary/caretaker etc, singer in the choir, pupil good at maths, pupil who doesn't like English, teaching assistant, etc.*)

(*Pull out different couples and ask..*)
Are they the same?
They all seem different but there is something that is the same about all of the people at the front. It's to do with the word I mimed for you.
(*Mime it again and take suggestions. If you have a school uniform it would help as a clue. When they guess, mime the word again slowly and write it on the flip chart.*)

All these people are different but they all **be – long** to _____ school. (**Thank participants and let them sit down.**)
What was the same? (*As they reply be – long, get them to mime the word.*) What does **be – longing** mean? (*Work together, play together, look out for each other, respect and care for each other, feel at home, sort out arguments, etc.*)

Stand up if you belong to class __.
What do you do? (*pupils respond be – long to…*) (*Repeat for the choir, the football team, other school/family groups, outside activity groups.*)

Some of us **be-long** to more groups than others but all of us **be-long** somewhere and are needed by other people and we need them too.

Why? What do we all do? — **Be-long**

Prayers and Thinking

In a time of silence, I am going to ask different groups to stand/raise their hands. When it 's your group's turn, look around and think about all the other people who belong to your group. Be glad that you belong and are part of it. Some of you might like to pray for anyone in your group who is ill or unhappy. When I say '**I'm glad I belong**' sit down/put your hand down. (*Call each class/year group in turn.*)

Quote for the day

All the lonely people, where do they all come from? All the lonely people, where do they all belong?'
John Lennon (1940–1980) *Eleanor Rigby*

Faith links

Christian
Life of the early
Church
Acts 2

Buddhist
The Sangha, one
of the 3 Jewels

Branching out

 Make a chart of all the different groups pupils belong to in and out of school.

 In groups, each with a jigsaw that has had one piece removed and put in a tin (secretly). Make jigsaw and find missing piece. Point out that the piece that 'belonged' fitted perfectly and completed the picture.

 Make up a jingle to advertise a group you belong to, e.g. football supporter, fan club, cubs, guides. Recite for class to guess what you belong to.

Someone, somewhere needs you

(Blast of music.) Welcome to tonight's **'Where does that go?'** Show. Once again we will be looking at groups of objects and deciding where they belong. I am your host for the evening – and now meet my assistants; ———— *(Call first pupil, comes in, bows, sits on first chair, while audience applauds.) (Repeat for assistants 2–4.)*

Again tonight, a group of objects will be passed along our conveyor belt to a waiting tray. *(Ask for a volunteer to stand at the end of the table with a tray to receive the objects.)* Watch carefully, it is up to you, our audience, to decide which belong together and will stay on the tray, and which one has to go.

(Cue quieter music). First up tonight we have … *(List objects slowly and deliberately. They are passed along the table to the tray.) (Cut music at last object.)*

That's our first group. Now it's up to you. What do you think? When I hold up each article you must tell me **'belong'** or **'go'** *(Hold up each article. If it's 'belong' leave on the tray, if 'go' put on tray on the table.) (As you hold up each article, someone write it on flip chart.) (Hold up 'belong' tray.)* Why do these things belong? *(e.g. all things to write with.) (Bracket list on flip chart and write group title.)*

Now for our second group. *(Cue music.) (Repeat as before and for all groups of objects.)*

Well that's our last belonging group for tonight. You have been a superb audience. *(Member of 'audience' calls out 'What about the tray on the table?')* *(Leader picks up tray from table.)* These are just the things that don't belong. We only have 4 belonging trays each week. This isn't a belonging tray? *(*Audience caller – 'Oh yes it is')*

Leader – Oh no it isn't *(Repeat panto style + pupils.)*
Leader – OK, you show me then. Why do they all belong? *(Pupils to reveal they are all china/crockery.)*

Well isn't that amazing! To think I thought they were just the odd ones out. It just goes to show everything belongs in a group somewhere, the ____, ____, *(List all the tray groups.)*

And as you go home tonight, remember you belong somewhere special too. Someone, somewhere needs you *(point round audience).* *(Short blast of music. Encourage applause.)*

(Come out of role.) I wonder what groups do we belong to? I belong to ———————— *(Give examples of groupings you belong to.)* What do you belong to? *(Take suggestions – family, school, groups of friends, Guides, Brownies, Cubs, Beavers.)* You are important to those groups. What did our games show leader say?

Someone, somewhere needs you.

All together now

Many pieces make a whole

YOU WILL NEED

2 large sheets of paper, a marker pen, a pair of scissors and Blu-Tack, the help of another teacher

Today's assembly is about working together. A school is a place where lots of people work together. (**Draw an outline of a building. Write the name of the school above it. Explain that lots of different people work at school, all doing different things. Ask the children to name some of them. Draw stick people inside the school and write their names next to them.**)

Although all the different people do different jobs they all come together to make one school. It's a bit like a jigsaw, when all the bits fit together you get a whole picture. (**Explain you want to turn the picture into a jigsaw to** play a game with, but you will need some help. Cut it into six pieces.)

(*Give the pieces to another teacher to hide without you knowing where they have gone. Leave the room.*)

(*On your return, ask for help to make the jigsaw. The children can give clues, take you to each piece or find each one for you. As each piece is found thank each child for helping you and working with you.*)

(*As each piece is found, Blu-Tack them onto another piece of paper to build up the jigsaw. When it is finished, ask which piece and whose help was the most important. After hearing pupils' comments, show that every piece is as important as the others.*) If you take any one away the picture cannot be finished. School is the same. Every single person is important and if we all work together like the jigsaw pieces then we make a happy whole school.

Prayers and Thinking

Close your eyes and think about the story you have just heard.

Help us to learn to work together and support each other. Help us to learn that as a team, we can do so much more than if we only think of ourselves. Amen.

Open your eyes. Turn to the people sitting either side of you and shake hands with them. Try your best to work as a team today

Quote for the day

The one who plants and the one who waters have a common purpose, and each will receive wages according to the labour of each.
Corinthians 3: 8

Faith links

Christian
The labourers in the vineyard
Matthew 20: 1–16

Muslim
Muhammad and his companions share the work on a journey

Branching out

 Play 'chain link' where three pupils hold hands and have to complete an obstacle course without breaking the chain.

 Friends make paper chains of people holding hands. Write words on them that describe why they like working together.

 Pupils make their own jigsaws of people working together from drawings or photos. They can then play the jigsaw game they saw in assembly.

Farmer's summer holiday

There was once a farmer **(put on cap)** who worked hard digging and weeding **(mime actions)** and sowing seeds **(seeds crouch down at the front)**. The farmer had two friends to help him. First there was the sun who shone down on the farm **(pupil holds up paper sun)** and kept the soil and the seeds warm. The other friend was the rain cloud **(pupil holds up paper rain cloud)** who kept the seeds watered and made sure they were never thirsty. Together they worked as a team **(all shake hands)** they helped the seeds grow **(farmer weeds, sun shines round the seeds, rain waters the seeds, the seeds gradually stand up)** and made sure there was a good harvest of corn.

But one year, just before harvest time, the farmer decided he had had enough of work and packed his suitcase and went away on holiday. **(Put on sun hat, pick up suitcase and walk off waving.)** The sun and rain were left on their own to do their work. The sun shone and the rain rained **(mime actions)** but without the farmer to do the weeding the seeds started to grow. **(Partially stand up.)** They soon got choked by weeds and died. **(Seeds mime choking and then crouch down again.)** This made the sun and the rain feel very angry with the farmer. **(Farmer returns with suitcase, sun and rain shake their fists at him.)**

The next year the sun was still feeling angry with the farmer **(shakes fist)** and thought if he can have a holiday so can I. So he went away leaving the farmer and the rain cloud to do all the work. **(Sun puts on sun hat, picks up suitcase and walks off waving.)** The farmer worked hard weeding **(mime)** and the

rain kept the seeds watered **(mime)** but without the warm sun the seeds did not grow. This made the farmer and the rain cloud very angry with the sun. **(Sun returns with suitcase, farmer and rain shake their fists at him.)**

The next year the rain cloud was feeling angry with the farmer and the sun **(shakes fist)** and so he went away leaving them to do all the work. **(Put on sun hat, pick up suitcase and walk off waving.)** The farmer worked hard weeding and the sun warmed the seeds and they started to grow **(rise up slightly)**, but without the rain the corn became thirsty and withered and died. **(Fall down.)** This made the farmer and the rain cloud very angry. **(Shake fists.)**

The next year, the sun and the rain cloud and the farmer started to argue about who would go on holiday and who should stay behind and work. **(Mime argument.)** All this time God had been watching what had been going on and he felt fed up with what he saw. **(Voice booms out on the microphone - 'Oy you lot! Stop all that arguing. You're meant to be friends aren't you? I didn't spend all my time creating you to fall out! I made you to work as a team. It's about time you realised how much you need each other. You want a good harvest don't you? Well you can't do it on your own. So you'd better start working together. Now hurry up and make friends before I have to come down there and sort you lot out!')** The three friends felt very silly after they had heard what God had to say. They realised he was right, shook hands and worked together to have the best harvest they had ever had **(mime)**. Then after all their work was done they went on holiday… together. **(All leave with case, waving.)**

Excuses! Excuses!

Always an excuse

YOU WILL NEED
Flip chart and pen

Gary belonged to a football team called 'Legs Eleven'. **('Legs eleven are the best. We make mincemeat of the rest!' Encourage the audience to clap and join in.)** Gary was the goalkeeper for 'Legs Eleven'. He was a great goalie, but was often late for training, or didn't turn up at all. He always had an excuse. Like, 'the dog had to go to the vets, or the car had a flat tyre, or there was a terrible traffic jam...' The rest of the team began to get fed up.

One Saturday, 'Legs Eleven' had a very important match against 'Kicker Kings'. It was an away game. The team and supporters were really excited about it. **(Repeat chant.)** They all made sure they went to bed early the night before to get plenty of rest for the big game. Well, all except Gary, that is. He went out as usual and didn't go to bed until late. He fell sound asleep. **(Snores.)** In the morning, when the team and supporters gathered to wait for the coach **(Chant.)** there was no sign of Gary. The captain phoned his house. **(Ring! Ring!)** No answer. Gary was still fast asleep **(snores)**. The team had to leave without him. They were furious. How could he let them down like this!

At the match the supporters did their best to cheer the team along. **(Chant.)** One of the other players took Gary's place. But after an injury in the first half, 'Legs Eleven' were down to ten men. Amazingly they still held the game to a draw. **(Cheer.)** When Gary woke up, he knew his team would be angry and was worried they'd drop him. He'd need a good excuse this time to keep out of trouble. He rushed to meet the coach when it got back. 'I'm sorry I missed the match,' he said. 'It won't happen again. You see, the problem was...' 'We don't want to hear any more of your excuses,' interrupted the captain. 'You're right it won't happen again.'

'Legs Eleven' thrashed the 'Kicker Kings' at the replay the following week. **(Chant.)** Gary watched the match from the side. He wouldn't be needing anymore excuses for a long time. Why not?

Prayers and Thinking

(Write the word EXCUSE in large letters on a flip chart. Tear it off. Hold it in front of you so that your face is hidden behind it, and then look out from the side. Do this a couple of times.)

Have you ever hidden behind an excuse?

Think or pray about being braver next time.

(Leave time for stillness, thinking and praying.)

Quote for the day
And oftentimes excusing of a fault
Doth make the fault the worse by the excuse.
William Shakespeare (1564-1616) *King John* Act 1V Sc 2

Faith links

Christian
The banquet excuses
Luke 14: 12–24

Sikh
Man is an 'action being' (Karma Yogi) working for mankind not self

Branching out

 Role play the story about Gary and 'Legs Eleven.' Expand the role play to include how the different team members and supporters felt. Use thought bubbles to record their feelings.

 Antique hallmarks point out the genuine from a fake. Reasons come from the heart, but excuses come from the head. Design hallmarks to tell false excuses from real reasons.

 Make some collages to illustrate the meaning behind the sayings – a flimsy, lame, weak, thin, feeble, poor, and silly excuse.

All the excuses in the book

PREPARATION NEEDED

Table with scientific equipment set out like a lab.

a large transparent container and a spoon

a set of 5 opaque containers, with the labels facing away from the audience-

- worries (contains little worried faces)
- words (speech bubbles)
- lies (twisted shapes)
- sorries – fake (tears)
- truth (empty)

white coat
big glasses, (optional)
wild wig! (optional)

a ring binder of blank OHT transparencies, labelled 'Bumper Book of Excuses'

an OHT pen

flip chart and pen for the prayer

WHAT TO DO

Narrator takes role of the professor or talks a pupil through this

(Put on costume. Rattle a few pieces of equipment, pour from one test tube into another, etc.) My name is Professor Thinkemup the famous inventor. I hear you need some good excuses for not handing in your homework on time. Well let me tell you …I have invented every excuse in the book! *(Hold up 'Bumper Book of Excuses'.)*

With your help as my expert assistants *(point to audience)*, I am sure we can make up some wonderful excuses that will really work. We'll fool everyone won't we? And keep ourselves out of trouble. After all that's what we want excuses for isn't it? *(Rattle equipment.)* Now let's see, what sort of excuses shall we start with? Any ideas? *(If anyone offers honesty at this point – dissuade them! You can return to them later. As each excuse is suggested, consult the book.)* Just a minute that excuse isn't in here. I'd better write it down. *(Write each one on a new OHT. Try to get a variety, e.g., the dog ate it, I had a tummy ache, my mum didn't remind me… someone's taken it out of my bag…you know the sort of thing!)*

Right! *(Close the book.)* We've got a whole load of new excuses here. Let's start making them up. *(Put out a large transparent container and a spoon.)* Who wants to come and help? *(Select four pupils. Each pupil takes the ingredient you give them and stirs it in the container.)* Now, what are excuses made up of? Oh yes, they always start with these *(Take out some worried faces out of a tin marked WORRIES.)* Can you see what they are? Did you know this is where excuses begin? Next we'll need these… *(Hold up container marked 'WORDS' Ask helper to tip them in.)* There are always plenty of words in excuses. We'll need one or two of these as

well. *(Take out a few twisted shapes from a container marked LIES.)* And a few of these. *(Hold up tin of SORRIES.)* Just a minute, let me make sure we've got the right tin. Yes, that's right. 'Fake' sorries. Not real ones. I mean when you make up an excuse you're not 'really' sorry are you? *(Tip in shapes.)*

There we are… worries, words, lies and fake 'sorries'. Everything that goes into a load of excuses. Give it a good stir. Finished! Just a minute… there's a tin left. We must have missed something out. *(Open up TRUTH.)* Oh… there's nothing in here. It's empty. What does it say on the label? Truth? Oh well, we don't want any of that do we? I mean these are not real excuses are they? There's no truth in them. We're making them up!

Now let's look at the different excuses we've made. *(Hold up book.)* We really have got all the excuses in the book now. You could try some of them out in school. *(Flick through the book.)* Oh no! Wait a minute. Something's wrong here. *(Take out a transparency. Hold it up and read it.)* That's no good! You can see straight through it! *(Do the same with another.)* This next one's see through too. *(Take them all out.)* They're all the same. Every single excuse! You can see straight through them all. No one will ever believe these! *(Collapse on the desk and groan.)*

(Take off coat.) Silly old Professor Thinkemup! He's got it all wrong hasn't he? Why do you think his excuses don't work? Is it right to try and do what he does? Why not? How do other people feel when they see through an excuse? What do they feel about the person giving the excuse?

Two carrier bags

Four strong walls

YOU WILL NEED

Flip chart and a marker pen – and if possible two carrier bags

Ask the pupils if they have ever seen anyone in their local town who is homeless. How do they feel when they see someone like that?

(Draw a picture of, or hold up, two carrier bags.) Explain that one woman, Ethel, has no house – just two carrier bags. What do they think is in them?

Discuss with the pupils what she might have with her and why she might have them.

Every night Ethel sleeps in a shop doorway. What do they think it's like sleeping there?

When she sleeps, Ethel dreams of where she used to live. She dreams of

four strong walls to keep her safe **(Draw a large square on a flip chart.)**

Ask pupils to come and add items to the picture, e.g. windows, door, roof, chimney, saying why Ethel needs them, e.g. to keep out the rain, let in light.

Admire the house and its features when it is finished.

Then explain when Ethel wakes in the morning, the house was just a dream.

All she really has are the two carrier bags. How do the pupils think she feels?

Explain that there some organisations that work with the homeless so that they do not have to sleep on the streets.

Maybe they will be able to help Ethel. Make a list of the things they might do.

Prayers and Thinking

Invite the children to close their eyes and draw a house for Ethel in their minds.

Let us pray and think about Ethel finding a real home like the one you have drawn. Let's remember to say thank you to the people who work with the homeless, so that no one has to sleep in doorways or be cold, lonely, hungry or afraid.

Amen

Quote for the day

A man travels the world over in search of what he needs and returns home to find it.
George Moore (1852-1933) *The Brook Kerith*, Ch 11

Faith links

Christian
Birth of Jesus in a stable
Luke 2: 1–20

Jewish
The building of a sukkah

Branching out

Find out about organisations such as Shelter or the Salvation Army on the Internet.

Display a silhouette figure with two bags. On the bags write homelessness. To the left add words and pictures about a past life, on the right ideas for a more positive future.

Role-play a night for Ethel in a shop doorway, including the reaction of people passing by and those who move her on.

I wasn't always like this

PREPARATION NEEDED

Two carrier bags
containing:

an old coat
newspaper
string
an old hat
old shoes
photos of a family
group and a house in
an old envelope
an old blanket or
sleeping bag

WHAT TO DO

How this assembly is
delivered depends on
your confidence and
teaching style.

'Teacher in role' does
not take great dramatic
skill, but you need to
feel comfortable.

If this is not for you then
the items in the bag can
be talked about without
going into role or worn
by someone else.

(If possible sing or listen to 'Streets of London' by Ralph McTell before the main part of the assembly begins. Then hold up the two carrier bags and ask the audience to guess what might be inside. Take out the old coat. Talk about what it looks like, old/ dirty/torn. Who might it belong to? Casually slip it on. Next take out the string. Ask what it might be for. Tie it round yourself as a belt for the coat.)

(Talk about the shoes, what they look like, worn/sole coming off. Gradually begin to assume the role as you slip on the shoes.) They're not much good these shoes, they are always letting in the rain. My feet get so cold and wet. And this coat's not much good either. **(Stuff the newspaper inside the coat.)** It gets so cold on the streets at night.

(Put on the hat.) I try to keep warm but it's not easy. **(Begin to walk around the room, talking as you go. Walk in a hunched up way, pulling your coat around you, shivering from the cold.)**

(Wipe your nose on your sleeve.) They call me the bag lady, but my name's Ethel. Nobody calls me Ethel. Nobody wants to talk to me. They move away as soon as they see me.

(Pull out the envelope of photographs.) I wasn't always like this you know. Oh I had a family once. Look! **(Hold up the photo. Walk amongst the children if possible.)**

There we all are at … (whatever the photo represents). It was a grand day that. We were so happy. All together as a family. There's mum, dad… me. Can't believe it now, can you? It was only later when things started to go wrong and I ended up like this."

(Hold up the photo of a house.) Look! I didn't always live on the streets you know. **(Carry on walking round.)** I had a house once, just like you, with my own bedroom and everything.

(Begin to move back to the front.) I didn't always live in doorways you know. I bet you've seen me there though haven't you? **(Wrap the blanket around yourself.)** I've got a blanket to keep me warm. Try to keep the wind off, get a bit of shelter. Time to try and get some sleep now. But sometimes I get moved on. Nobody wants me around.

(Look at the photos again before putting them away in the envelope.) Got to keep these safe. They're all I've got left now. **(Look at the audience.)** I did have a family once, just like you. **(Curl up for the night.)** I wasn't always like this. **(Pause and stay curled up for a short while. Then quietly move and take off the items used and put them back in the bag, without saying anything. Now talk to the children out of role. Have they seen anyone like Ethel? How might she feel?)**

A leading light?

I'll lead...you follow

Prayers and Thinking

Have you ever played the game 'Follow my Leader'? (*Ask pupils to explain the rules.*) That sounds fun. Let's have a game of this now.

Who wants to be the leader? Oh dear, so many hands have gone up. How do I choose? Tell you what I'll choose... **me**, **I'll** be the leader. No it's no good moaning. **I've** decided so there! And because **I'm** the leader, what **I** say goes.

And you (*point out 6 pupils*) can be my followers. No ... no one else ... **I'm** the leader remember everyone has to do what **I** say.

Now you followers have to do exactly what **I** tell you to do. You **must** do what **I** say at all times. That's how it works. **I** lead and you follow.

Now which way shall we go? No, no you don't have a say...**I'm** not listening to you...**I'm** the person who decides things round here. **I'm** the leader remember. You do what **I** say.

I know... we'll go this way. (*Start to lead group around the room.*) No...wait a minute... **I've** changed my mind...we'll go this way. (*Lead in a different direction.*) No ...hang on this way looks best after all. (*Change direction again, and carry on doing this for a few more times, getting everyone into a muddle.*)

WHOAH...Stop everyone! You're getting in such a mess! You're just not doing it right! What's wrong with you! It can't be that difficult to follow such a **brilliant** leader as **me**! This mess can't be **my** fault can it? What do you mean...it is **my** fault? I don't understand. What was I doing wrong? What sort of things should a leader do?

Sit quietly and close your eyes.

Try and see a picture in your mind of a snowy day. Walk across the deep crunchy snow. Stop and turn round. Look at the footprints you have made. Someone later might follow these and step where you have stepped.

Always try to make sure the footsteps you leave will make a good path for someone else to follow.

Quote for the day

And if the blind lead the blind, both shall fall into the ditch.
Matthew 13:14

Faith links

Christian and Jewish

Moses leads his people over the Red Sea
Exodus 14

Branching out

 Look at signs and symbols used in different religions – e.g. Jewish: mezuzah, Buddhist: prayer wheel, Muslim: mihrab, Sikh: five 'KS', Christian: cross.

 Divide into small teams, each team devises a map and/or trail to help another group of people follow a route.

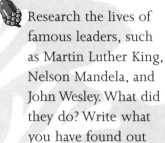 Research the lives of famous leaders, such as Martin Luther King, Nelson Mandela, and John Wesley. What did they do? Write what you have found out inside footsteps.

In someone else's footsteps

PREPARATION NEEDED

Plan a secret route around the room with key points to act as markers and changes in direction

paper
marker pens
Blu-Tack
scissors
to make signs and clues

a colleague or pupil volunteer to act as your follower (they will have to wait for a while outside the room)

further volunteers to place signs and to act as guides

We are going to think about what makes a good leader. *(Ask for a helper.)* We are going to go on a journey. I know where I want us to go so I want you to follow me and try and step exactly where I step. Do what I do. *(Walk in a straight line with volunteer following.)* That's right. Let's walk a different path *(Walk a wobbly path with volunteer following.)* Well done, it was a bit harder, but you did fine.

Now I want you to follow in my footsteps **after** I have made them. You can watch what I do, then try and follow in my footsteps afterwards. *(Walk a zigzag path. Volunteer waits and watches, then repeats it as best as they can.)* Not bad! But it was much harder to do wasn't it?

I want you to leave the room for a moment while I make a new path for you to follow. *(Volunteer leaves. Leader walks a clear route round the room, touching obvious points such as windows and doors, before changing direction. Then fetches volunteer.)* Now I want you to try and follow the path I made for you when you were out of the room. Can you see it? Do you know which way to go? No? Oh dear... I'm not much of a leader am I? Maybe if I'd thought about what you needed a bit more, left you some clues, a few signs to follow, it would have been better. Let's do it again, this time I'll try and help you on your journey and leave some clues. *(Volunteer leaves the room.)*

(Turn to the audience.) Do you remember which way I went? How can I help my follower know what to do? Travelling can be scary, if you don't know which way to go. I want

him/her to feel happy and safe. Use pupils' suggestions to create a set of paper clues – e.g. arrows, footprints, map, written instructions, and place people acting as guides at key points along the way. With the help of different pupils, lay a clear trail for the volunteer to follow.

(Fetch the volunteer back in.) This time you won't get lost. I promise you. You can do it, I know you can. I've tried to think what you will need and have left a trail for you to follow. If you're not sure what to do, I have asked people to help you along the way, listen to and use what they say. *(With the assistance of clues, guides and the audience if needed, the volunteer is supported along the path. Be there to greet the volunteer at the end.)* Well done, you made it, you were amazing. Let's give this weary traveller and everybody who helped a huge clap.

Can you see how much easier it was for **name of pupil** to find his/her way by following a trail? **Name** was able to listen to and get help from other people too.

You see a leader may not always be there to show people the way. But if he or she is a good leader, that won't matter. He/she will leave a trail and encourage other people to help. Together they help people do things for themselves. Famous leaders in history have always done this, people like Jesus, Buddha, and Muhammad left their own trail. They talked to people about their ideas, then left stories, signs and guides to help people on their way. People still think about their ideas and follow their trails today.

Full of promise

I give you my word

YOU WILL NEED

Flip chart, marker pens, jar of coffee from staff room, mug

(Hold up the coffee jar.) What do you think is in this jar?... How do you know? **(Encourage the answer 'it says on the label'.)** Absolutely right! The makers give us their word, they write on the label what is inside **(Tear off the label, hand it to a pupil.)** The makers give you their word. Here you look after it. What does 'Give you their word' mean? (promise) You know that if you put it in your mug **(pour granules in mug)** you will have...? Tea ? **(Pupils to respond 'no!')** Chocolate? **(No!)** What will you have then?

(*Write MY WORD at corner of the flip chart so that everyone sees. Tear it off and. Say...) I give you my word that assembly will not last longer than 2 hours! **(Give it to a pupil.)** Would you **keep** my promise for me please.

(Repeat * for the following statements): You can have 10 minutes free choice one day next week; David Beckham (or other celebrity) will come to visit you next week; **(To colleague)** I will provide biscuits for break time; it will not rain for six weeks.

(Go back to the coffee jar.) What would you do, if when you opened the jar, a pile of small stones fell out? **(Encourage response – 'Take it back / complain'.)** Why? (Response – because it wasn't what it said on the jar/they didn't keep their promise.)

(Ask assembly.) Who's got my WORDS? Do any of you think I ought to have them back because you know I can't keep them? Let's look at them again. What did I promise _____? Do you think I can keep that promise? **(Discuss each WORD. If you can keep it , why/not, etc. Take back the promise if you cannot keep it. Say...)** I cannot keep this promise, it would be broken. **(Rip the paper in two.)**

It's important we only make promises we can and will keep. Any ideas why it is important? (Response – people depend/rely on our promises, people will be hurt/upset, it's like telling lies, etc.) What a muddle everyone would be in if jars and tins didn't keep the promise on the label; if baked beans had a custard label on or mustard had a jam label. **(On the flip chart, list promises we make to each other.)**

When I gave you MY WORDS what did I ask you to do? (Response – 'keep it'.) Can **you** keep **my** promises? No I think I had better have them all back and make sure I keep them myself. **(Repeat them.)**

Prayers and Thinking

(Write MY WORD on the flip chart.) Think about the promises you make to people and promise yourself that you will keep them. Those who believe in God thank Him that He has given His word to always be with you.

Quote for the day
Boldness is an ill keeper of promise.
Francis Bacon (1561–1626) *Essays*, 12, 'Of Boldness'

Faith links

Christian
Promise of heaven
John 14: 1–3

Jewish
God's promise to Abraham
Genesis 15

Branching out

 Collect junk mail or advertisements. Think about what are they are promising?

 Ask Guides, Brownies, Beavers, Cubs, to share their promises with the class. Compose a class promise.

 Write a guarantee for an everyday object. Read for others to guess the object.

A gentleman's agreement

(Explain you will be needing some volunteers to work in your factory. It's a very important job and you promise to pay your workers. The job will be bundling or stacking in groups of five, to sell to teachers for maths.)

*Who will be my first worker? (Take first volunteer, make sure they understand what to do.) You start when the whistle blows. When it blows again you stop work. I promise to pay you one 'sweet' for each 'bundle'. (Check they are happy with that.)

(Blow whistle. Encourage assembly to cheer him/her on. After short time blow whistle again. Explain worker is doing well but the job won't get done in time, you need another volunteer.)*

(Repeat from * to * until three volunteers are working.)

(Blow whistle for workers to stop. Call one more volunteer, explain job and agree to pay them 'a fair wage'. Blow whistle. When final worker has made one bundle blow whistle again to stop.)

That looks as if we have enough. Well done. Now it's pay time.

First worker (Ask assembly to count bundles with you. Count and pay relevant wage, asking assembly how much? Are they sure? What was it you promised? etc.)

Second worker (Count, but refuse to pay because the bundles aren't tidy enough. Move on to third worker, ignoring any protests, count and pay as for number one.)

Fourth worker (One bundle, well done I think a fare wage is a packet of... hand him/her the small packet or 20p making sure the assembly can hear and see what you are doing.) (Thank your workers and ask them to sit down.)

(Ask for comments on how you run your factory. They will probably mention the unfair payment system. Point out that you had made promises. Ask what they were).

Workers 1–3: 1 sweet per bundle
Worker 4: a fair wage

(Call out each worker, one at a time and ask if you kept your promise to that person.)
How did I keep/break my promise? How did that make ——— feel? (Decide whether to give a happy or angry mask.) (With worker 3 ask...) Do you think ——— will want to work for me again? Will he tell other people to come and work in my factory? It's important for everyone to keep their promises no matter what anyone else thinks.

(Ask for suggestions of promises made in school or in the village/town.) What happens when those promises are broken? Breaking promises makes people angry and unhappy.

Breaking up and making up

A circle of friends

YOU WILL NEED

Flip chart, a pen and a pair of scissors

Do you know what this shape is? **(Draw a circle then cut it out.)** Circles are a very special shape, aren't they? They go all the way round without any gaps or breaks. **(Run a finger round the circle.)** Can you draw one in the air just like mine? It's a strong shape and is hard to break. **(Pull at the shape.)** But once a crack appears... **(make small rip)** it is not so strong and can be pulled apart. **(Rip circle in two.)**

Let's make another circle – a circle of friends. I'll need eight people altogether. Now shake hands and then link arms to make a circle. This circle of friends is just like the ones we drew. It has no breaks in it at all. When they walk round together, it's a bit like a wheel turning.

Do you remember how strong our circle was? If friendship is strong like that, it can be hard to break too. Let's see if these friends can stick together

when I try and break them up. **(Pull at the circle.)** No it's no good, I can't do it! They're sticking together.

Did you notice that when the circle turned, all the friends went the same way? What would happen if some of them went a different way? Let's see. **(Ask half to go one way and the rest in the opposite direction.)** Oh dear it isn't such a smooth circle is it? **(Pull the circle apart.)** And now it's broken! Sadly friends and families don't always stay together. They sometimes split up, just like this circle did. This can be very difficult to cope with. How do you think people might feel when this happens?

Sometimes it's possible to patch things up **(circle shakes hands)** and get together again. **(Link arms again.)** But sometimes the break can't be fixed **(part circle)** and people split up and go their different ways. **(All walk in different directions.)** It can be hard to accept this when it happens. But in time, other friendships start **(put into two smaller circles)** and new circles of friends are made. **(Link arms and circles turn.)**

When families and friends fall out it sounds like this. (Play discordant notes on piano or recorder.)

When they try to make friends, they try to get back in tune.

Listen quietly to this music and think and pray about your family and friends.

(Play peaceful harmonious music.)

Quote for the day
Quarrels would not last so long if the fault were only on one side.
Duc de La Rochefoucauld (1613–1680) *Les Maximes* 496

Faith links

Christian
The disciples argue about which one of them is the greatest
Luke 9: 43–50

Hindu
Brahma, Vishnu and the pillar of fire

Branching out

 Use dance to explore the ideas in 'Circle of Friends'. How can the feelings involved in 'falling out', 'breaking apart' and 'repairing and rebuilding' be shown?

 Make a display showing a 'war of words' using oppositional phrases and soldiers on a battle field. Talk about how wars start and the consequences of these.

 Explore division in maths through partitioning, division sums and dividing shapes into fractions. What do you need to do to reverse a division?

The first move

PREPARATION NEEDED

Picture symbols for
• friendship
• argument
• anger
• bravery

recorder
xylophone
tambourine

chalk or a strip of paper
or length of rope to
make line

WHAT TO DO

This assembly is for a
class or group to
rehearse and present as
a narrated dance.

The assembly leader is
the narrator.

The narrator can also
play the recorder and
tambourine or these can
be played by other staff
and/or pupils.

Ask someone to hold up
the picture symbols at
the correct points in the
dance.

(Pupils line up side by side with their arms linked, facing the audience.) Usually people get on well with each other. *(Recorder plays happy tune. Pupils move about shaking hands with each other. Recorder stops and pupils move back into their line.)*

But when people fall out, *(shake tambourine and pupils move about shaking fists, sticking tongues out, pushing and jostling against each other)* they sometimes gang up in groups *(pupils form two separate huddles/scrums and whisper to one another. Beat quiet continuous rhythm tam, tam-tam, tam tam-tam)* and take sides against each other. *(Pupils split up into two lines facing each other, as tambourine gets louder. Make one loud bang on tambourine. Pupils take two steps back, and then stand in silence facing each other.)*

It's as if a line has been drawn between them. *(Shake tambourine again as line is drawn or placed between the sides.)* Once the line is there, it can be difficult to cross back and make friends again. *(Play tam tam-tam rhythm again. One or two pupils from each side go up to line, but stop and look back at their gang, who call them back.)* They turn their backs on their old friends. *(Tambourine gets louder as pupils turn their backs to each other. Make one loud bang. Pupils stand back to back in silence.)*

Sometimes they shout at each other.

(Pupils turn and face each other. Facing partners shout oppositional words at each other. As each word is shouted they point angrily at each other across the line. The words might include yes/no, can/can't, is/isn't, did/didn't, will/won't, have/haven't, was/wasn't, shall/shan't. Alternate which side says the first word.) Then other people join in and a real war of words begins. *(Repeat sequence with whole sides pointing and chanting the words at each other in unison. After last word bang tambourine loudly. Pupils fold arms and stand facing each other in silence.)*

When it gets this bad, no one wants to give in. It's as if the two sides are stuck. No one wants to make the first move. But if just one person is brave enough. Look what happens. *(Play sliding sound on xylophone. One person steps forward and holds out hand across the line.)* Someone else will join them. *(Repeat sound. Opposite partner steps forward and they shake hands. Together they remove the line between the sides.)* And before you know it, the line that came between everyone has gone. *(All step forward, shake hands.)* And friendship can begin again. *(Recorder repeats tune played at the beginning. Pupils move about amongst each other, smiling and patting each other on the back. Then as music stops, they line up side by side again, link arms and bow.)*

Are you brave enough to make the first move?

Can I help you?

What's my job?

YOU WILL NEED

Flip chart with 2 columns headed **Experts** and **Workers,** marker pens

MIME SUGGESTIONS

policeman, road sweeper, a person who takes someone out in a wheelchair, playgroup leader, shopping for an elderly person, lollipop person

Leader: *(as a games show host)* Welcome to the TV show 'What's My Job'. Where volunteers from the audience come out and I tell them to mime a job that someone does to help in our (village/town/school). A panel of experts will try to guess what the person's job is. But to make it a bit more difficult the experts will not see the first mime. Someone else will come out and copy the mime for them to see.

Who will be on the first panel of experts? **(Choose three.)** Let's give them a clap. Now two volunteers to mime for us. **(Choose two.)** Give them a clap too.

Now our experts will go to the sound-proof room. **(Experts go out so they cannot** *see the first mime.)* And the first job is... *(Whisper to 1st volunteer, see list above. 1st volunteer mimes watched by volunteer 2, who is not told what to do.)*

(Leader to audience.) Hands up, but don't call out, if you think you know what he/she is doing. **(Call in the experts to watch second version. Volunteer 2 copies what he/she thinks volunteer 1 did. The panel have one guess each, to try to guess what it is. If one guesses, award a tick on the flip chart if not the workers get a tick. Choose new workers and panel, repeat two or three times.)**

(Ask.) Who thought it was easier to guess from the 1st mime? Why? **(Encourage because the 2nd person didn't know what they were miming.)** **(Sum up.)** Lots of people do things to help in our community that we don't know. Even if we see them we don't always recognise what they are doing because they often do it without telling anyone and without being paid.

What other jobs can you think of that people do to serve our school/village/town? **(Pupils come out and mime.)** In a moment of quiet, think of a job that needs doing. Could you do it?

Prayers and Thinking

(Draw round the hands of two or three pupils. Write give a hand to...)
Begin with arms folded, hands hidden. Think about the times we don't feel like helping others. Put your hands on you knees, think about all the people who need help far more than we do. Turn your hands face up and think of all the things you could offer to do for others or pray that you will be able to help someone.

Quote for the day

To give and not to count the cost...to labour and not to ask for any reward. Saint Ignatious Loyola (1491–1556) *Prayer for Generosity*

Faith links

Christian
The Good Samaritan
Luke 10: 25

Sikh
The Guru and the Water Carrier

Branching out

 Make a display 'I could give a hand to...' Draw round your hand, cut it out, write on it a person you could help and what you could do.

 Make a list of things to put in a surprise parcel to give to an elderly person, a sick child, someone who can't see.

 In groups mime things you could do to help at school, at home, in your town. Guess what the other groups are miming.

Spoons at a metre

PREPARATION NEEDED

6 dessertspoons each tied to the end of a metre stick

a bag of marshmallows or other suitable large sweets

three plates, a colleague primed to help you if necessary

flip chart divided into 2 columns

WHAT TO DO

Share the marshmallows between the 3 plates and place them on a table with a tablecloth (The idea of this challenge is for the pupils to realise that they need to think of others and 1) help push the marshmallow onto the spoon to feed each other 2) wait while one pair works at a time. It is easier with forks but not as safe!)

Who likes (marshmallows)? Good, because today we are having a Marshmallow Munch. Who would like to share my Marshmallow Munch? **(Choose six volunteers. Invite them to the front and stand three down each side of the table.)** You can eat from any plate when you are ready... **(As they go to eat, shout STOP!)** You aren't ready, you didn't think it was going to be that easy did you?

(Produce the long handled spoons and give them one each.) As I said you can eat from any plate but it's bad manners to eat with your fingers, you must use a spoon and you must hold the end of the stick. OK? Ready, steady, go! **(Encourage assembly to shout for a volunteer. Give a running commentary on what each person is doing 'She's nearly got it', 'Can't reach her mouth', 'He's going for the pink one', etc.) (If it looks as if someone has worked it out, stop them quickly or if no one comes up with a solution after a few minutes, stop them and say...)**

Well give them a clap for trying but it's not much of a meal if no one's eating anything. What about someone else coming to my marshmallow meal? **(Choose six more volunteers. Give them a minute or two to try. If someone works it out, stop the others and let them go ahead while you comment on what they are doing. If no one gets it ask the assembly for ideas. Try**

them. If it still is not solved, ask ...) Do you think it's possible? Do you think I could do it? ....Well it looks as if Mr/Ms _____ and I are going to have a feast. **(Colleague comes and you feed each other.) (Invite all pupils who tried, to come and have a marshmallow.)**

(Sum up) Why was it so difficult to eat the marshmallows? (Couldn't reach, couldn't pick them up.) When we were thinking of helping ourselves we got nothing, except more and more annoyed/frustrated. What made it possible? (When we fed each other.) When we stopped thinking about ourselves and served the other person, we both got marshmallows and both felt very happy.

What things could you offer to do for others who have difficulties? (e.g. back zip, buttons on cuffs, buttons at the back, tying shoelaces, on the PE apparatus, reading instructions.) **(List in first column.)**

What things do you need help with? **(List in second column.) (Look at the two columns and see which ones can be paired up.)**

Well that's a start. When we are doing things in school let's look out for different ways we can serve other people.

World

WOW! Wonder of wonders

Pretty maids all in a row

YOU WILL NEED

Flip chart and marker pens

(Ask the pupils for the name of a favourite flower or flower growing in their garden. As they name them draw a rough sketch and comment on the variety of flowers and shapes.)

Story: The castle gardens were magnificent. There were flowers everywhere, red, yellow, blue, purple and pink flowers. Visitors came and marvelled at all the different kinds of flowers, the *roses, tulips, hollyhocks* and *lupins.*

But it was a good job they couldn't hear what was going on in the flower bed by the pond. The flowers were arranging a beauty contest and they couldn't stop arguing. 'Well look at me,' said the lupin, 'I am so tall and slender I am bound to win.' **(Choose a pupil to be a tall lupin.)** 'What about my velvety skin,' said the rose, stroking her face, 'no one has a skin like mine, the judges are bound to choose me.' **(Choose a rose.)** 'Rubbish!' squeaked the tiny violet looking up at the tall flowers. 'My pretty face will be the winner.' **(Choose a tiny violet and line them all up.)**

Every day the flowers lined up (**organise the line**) and the arguments went on. **(Pushing and shoving, etc.)** One day the daisy looked up 'Who is going to be the judge? How will we know who is the most beautiful?' Now no one had really thought about that. After much discussion **(flowers in a huddle)** it was agreed **(flowers all shake hands)** that the next person who came along and said how beautiful a flower was would be the judge and that flower the winner. The flowers waited **(all line up straight)** hoping the visitors would choose them, but everybody just gazed and said 'What beautiful flowers!'

'Shh,' whispered the violet, 'someone's coming'. Along the path came John with his Gran. He stopped at the flowerbed. The flowers were so excited. 'Oh gran!' said John, 'Wow, look at that beautiful flower.' The flowers could hardly wait. 'That's a dandelion,' said gran. 'It's such a lovely yellow,' said John, and the rain is sparkling in its petals. The flowers could not believe it. **(Hands on hips.)** Dandelion! She was a weed! She hadn't even entered the contest. Dandelion smiled she didn't need a judge, she knew they were <u>all</u> amazing.

Prayers and Thinking

You need four or five sheets plain A4 paper scissors and Blu-Tack. *(Cut out either flower petals or stars. Ask for ideas of beautiful things to write or draw on them . Hand them to pupils from each year group.)*
We are going to be quiet. As we stick up each star/petal, picture all the beautiful things in our world. If you believe God made them, say thank you to Him.

Quote of the day
Beauty is eternity looking at itself in a mirror.
Kahlil Gilbran (1923)
The Prophet

Faith links

Christian
Christ's Nativity;
Angels appearing to the Shepherds
Luke 2: 8-20

Jewish
Hanukka

Branching out

 Wind sparkly thread round crossed twigs to make a spider's web. Thread on beads, hang them at the window to catch the light.

 Listen to Psalm 23, what 'beautiful places' are mentioned there? Draw them and imagine being there.

 Collect stones and put them in water or varnish them. Look at the colours and patterns in them.

Mirror image

PREPARATION NEEDED

A mirror type frame held by a pupil on each side

pictures of: a sunset, shining spider's web, starry sky

2 pictures of Rosie to fill the frame (a) looking glamorous (b) looking natural

a pupil to mime Rosie

hairbrush

make-up

gaudy top or shawl

strings of beads/hair slides etc.

'Voice off'

flip chart

(Introduce Rosie.) Rosie spends a lot of time looking in her special mirror and asking it questions. Do you know what she says? Let's practise so we can help her **(Practise *Mirror, mirror do your duty, tell me I'm a raving beauty*.)**

You've probably guessed Rosie was very vain. She was always fussing about how she looked. She wanted to be the most beautiful thing in the world. Everything else seemed very dull and ugly. Now Rosie had a special mirror. Each day she spent hours brushing her hair, **(brush hair)** putting on her make-up **(smear on make-up)** and dressing in her best clothes and all her jewelry **(dress up)**. Then she went to her mirror and said … **(Stand in front of frame.) (Repeat from* to *.)**

(Hold glam picture of Rosie in frame.) There in the mirror she saw herself looking really glamorous. She set off into town very pleased. People laughed as she went by. They're just jealous thought Rosie because they are so ugly, but she felt a bit uncomfortable. 'I'll just go and see my mirror,' she said. **(Repeat from * to *.)**

(Picture of spider's web in frame.) This time she didn't see herself but **(ask pupils)** a spider's web shining in the sun. 'Oh that's beautiful!' gasped Rosie. To her amazement the mirror spoke **(voice off)** † **Rosie, Rosie do your duty, Take a look at all my beauty** †**.** Rosie rushed into the garden, there were thousands of webs

covered in raindrops, sparkling in the sun. 'That's really beautiful,' sighed Rosie, 'I wish I was as beautiful as that'. She ran back in and went to her mirror **(* *)**

(Picture of sunset in frame. Ask pupils what she can see.) There in the mirror she saw a brilliant sunset. The mirror spoke again. († †**)** She ran to the window and looked up, sure enough it looked as if the sky was on fire. 'That's amazing! If only my hair shone like that,' thought Rosie. 'I'll go and ask my mirror.' **(* *)**

(Picture of a starry sky in frame.) Again Rosie didn't see herself. In the mirror was… **(Ask pupils.)** There were millions of twinkling stars. Rosie thought they were out of this world, she didn't know what to say. She turned to her mirror and what do you think? Before she had time to say anything, there she was, she could see herself again **(natural picture in frame)** with the stars and spiders' webs and sunset. The mirror spoke '**Rosie, Rosie now you know, That beauty's everywhere you go'.** Rosie looked in the mirror again then out of the window and suddenly, everything looked very beautiful.

(Ask pupils who they think could have been speaking to Rosie.)
Ask pupils for suggestions of other amazing things that the mirror could have shown Rosie.

What on earth...?

A load of rubbish

YOU WILL NEED

A rubbish bin, some newspaper, a flip chart and pen

Today we are going to talk 'rubbish'. **(Write this down.)** Yes that's right ...rubbish. **(Screw up some paper and throw it in the bin.)** As we are in school, we'll talk about the 3 Rs as well. **(Write these down.)** But these aren't the usual ones we talk about. No these are rubbish words too! **(Invite pupils out to throw more paper in the bin.)** But although they are rubbish words, they are important.

The problem with rubbish is that there is so much. **(More paper into the bin.)** Every time we buy new things like crisps or a toy, they come wrapped up. We only want the crisps or the toy. We don't want the rubbish, so we throw it in the bin. **(More paper into the bin.)**

But look what's happening to the bin...it's filling up. What will happen now? Yes the bin men take it, to the rubbish tip. But we make so much rubbish that these are getting full too, just like our bin. **(More paper into the bin.)** Soon there won't be anywhere to put our rubbish. Remember too that paper comes from trees. We cut down trees to make paper which we then just throw away!

We need to try and do something about this. That's where the 3 Rs come in. They stand for Reduce, Reuse and Recycle. Reduce means use less. How could we do this? **(E.g. try not to waste paper, say no when a shop offers you a bag.)** Reuse means use something again or mend something when it breaks. How could we do this? **(E.g. use both sides of your paper for drawing on.)** Recycle means making new things from rubbish. How could we do this? **(Don't throw newspapers away.)** **(Ask pupils to get them out of the bin and fold them up.)** What should we do now? (Take them to the paper bank to be made into more paper.) Let's all try to do something now. Let's talk and think Rubbish! What are you going to do?

Close your eyes and imagine a warm sunny day. You are walking in the woods. There is a gentle breeze. The leaves are fluttering and rustling in the breeze. Birds are singing from the treetops. Choose a tree and stand at the bottom. Look up into its tall branches. Put your arms around the trunk and give the tree a big hug. Remember you need the tree and it needs you. You are both part of the web of life. Let's not throw this away.

Amen.

Quote for the day

We are as much alive as we keep the earth alive.
Chief Dan George (1982) *My Spirit Soars*

Faith links

Christian
Francis Assisi and his 'Canticle of Brother Sun'

Jewish
Festival of Tu B'Shevat (New Year for Trees)

Branching out

Design some posters with catchy slogans that encourage people to think about the 3Rs of Rubbish. Display these around school.

Look at the process of recycling paper and how this helps to conserve trees. Try making your own paper.

Make a wall collage of a tree and the web of life. Use real objects from the environment, feathers, twigs, leaves, nuts.

The web of life

Trees are very beautiful things aren't they? **(Show images.)** But do you know how special they are? Let's make a tree to see if we can find out. **(Call out six children to make the shape of a tree. They should stand close together back to back and shoulder to shoulder in a circle to make the girth.)** This is the trunk. The tree's branches grow tall and wide. **(The children should stretch out their arms for the branches, their fingers for twigs.)** On the branches grow leaves, flowers and nuts. **(Give each pupil a leaf shape, flower, or a nut to hold in the fingers of one hand, leaving the other hand free.)** The tree helps other living things. Other creatures are joined to the tree in a web of life. **(Take a ball of string and tie it round the trunk of the tree. Then one at a time, hold up images of six different creatures that depend on trees asking the audience to identify them. Ask the individuals that answer to come out and hold up the picture they have identified standing around the tree but a few steps back from it. Stretch the string out from the tree to each 'creature' to hold and then stretch it back to one of the children representing the tree again. Each time ask / prompt the audience to realise the relationship between the tree and the creature as set out below.)**

The **beetles** live in the cracks in the trees, **caterpillars** live on the leaves, the **bees** drink the nectar from the flowers and help the nuts and berries grow, the **birds** eat the beetles and caterpillars and live in the branches, the **squirrel** eats the nuts and buries some of them in the ground for later. New baby trees grow from the nuts that they forget about and leave behind. **People** need trees too! Do you know why? Yes they use the wood to build houses and furniture. Yes they make paper, cardboard, newspapers and books from the wood. Yes they eat the berries, nuts and fruit that grow on the trees. But they need trees for something else too.

(Take a deep breath.) Can you do this? Well then you need to thank a tree! They help people breathe! You see trees need to breathe just like we need to. They don't have lungs, they breathe through tiny little holes in their leaves. And when they do this, they do something for us too. They clean the air – all the dirty air from factories, towns and cars – and give us nice clean air to breathe, instead of horrid, smelly polluted air. So you see people are joined to trees too. **(Link 'people' to the tree as before.)** In fact we are all joined together; people, insects, birds, animals, plants and trees – just like the threads in a spider's web. If one of us is hurt and pulls on the web, **(pull string)** we all feel it too. That's why we need to look after all living things.

You would think that as trees are so important, people would look after them better. Yet they seem to spend all their time chopping them down to make way for new houses, towns and roads. But when a tree dies, look what happens. **(Cut the string around the trunk and ask all the pupils to lie down.)** All the other creatures are affected too; their food and their homes have gone. Without trees they could die too. What about people? If we cut down too many trees, what could happen to us? That's why it is important not to do this and if we have to cut down a tree, to plant a new one in its place. We need to remember that people need trees; we are all part of the web of life.

The master touch

Sheer genius

YOU WILL NEED

a flipchart, red, black, green, orange, yellow, brown markers. Divide flipchart into 4 sections

Jake was visiting his Gran. He was collecting the acorns under the oak tree in her garden. **(Draw acorn where four sections meet.)** 'That's where this tree came from,' said his Gran. 'What, that huge tree from this little acorn?' he gasped, 'That's amazing!' He looked up at the tree, it was beautiful. **(Ask pupils to describe the tree, colours, acorns, leaves on the ground, etc. Draw in 1st section. Pupils come and colour in. Talk about what a beautiful picture it is.)**

After Christmas Jake went to see his Gran again. He ran into the garden to see the beautiful coloured oak tree. It had changed, it looked so different, but it was still very beautiful. **(Ask pupils to describe a winter tree, shapes and colour of the branches. Draw in 2nd section, pupils colour.)**

In the Spring, when Jake went to visit his Gran, he didn't know what to expect. **(Ask what pupils think he will see. Draw and colour tree in bud.)** Yes there it was, another new and beautiful picture. **(Describe picture.)** 'It's just like that tree is an artist,' said Jake, 'and is painting different pictures.' 'Well,' said Gran, 'it hasn't finished yet; you come and see me again in the summer.'

As soon as school finished Jake and his mum went to see Gran. Gran covered his eyes. 'Come and see the last picture,' she said. They walked into the garden, Jake held his breath, excited to see what the tree would look like now. **(Ask what he will see, draw and colour bright green leaves and sun.)** Jake ran under the tree and looked up at the sun sparkling through the leaves. 'This artist is a genius!' he laughed. There are thousands of pictures like the oak tree, in our world that no one has painted. What others can we think of? **(See prayers and thinking.)**

Prayers and Thinking

(Draw five or six hanging picture frames. Ask for suggestions of beautiful things in our world, write/draw them in the picture frames.)

Imagine we are in an art gallery, walking along looking at the pictures. As I point to each one we stop and think about how beautiful it is, the colours and shapes. Decide which one you would like to take home and hang on your wall. Tell the artist what a genius he is. You might believe the artist is God.

(Point to each picture in turn and name it... Ask pupils to choose their picture and think what a genius the artist is.)

Quote for the day

Genius does what it must and talent what it can.

Meredith Owen (1831–1891) *Last Words of a Sensitive Second Rate Poet*

Faith links

Christian and Jewish
Creation
Genesis 1

All faiths
Creation stories

Branching out

 Collect twigs, stones, moss, grasses and make a plate garden/world.

 Watch clouds. What pictures and shapes can you see? Tell stories about them.

 Research old ideas/maps of what the world was like.

Out of the dust

1. Collection of scrap paper (tissue, coloured, newspaper, etc)

   background paper on an easel,

   gluestick

2. Box of junk,

   string, elastic bands

3. 1 bin liner,

   collection of carrier bags,

   sticky tape,

   flip chart,

   marker pens,

   whistle,

   5 minute timer or stopwatch

WHAT TO DO

Arrange the three groups of materials on three separate tables, with 3 creators at each table. Divide assembly into 3 groups to encourage the 'creators'.

Indicate the first group and say that they are going to create a collage picture. The second group is going to create a model and the third group is going to create a costume for one of them to wear. The assembly groups can offer advice and support. The hardest part is they only have (5) minutes from the countdown and they must stop making and shouting when you blow the whistle. Ask for volunteer timekeeper.

Whole assembly begins countdown from 10. Start stopwatch. Blow whistle after (5) minutes.

Divide flip chart into four columns. Tell them this is for the judges' marks. They are all going to judge the creations:
1st for imagination (being different)
2nd for use of materials
3rd for the finished product (picture, model garment).

They give marks out of 5 by calling out a number. (You decide the average! Write it in the group's column.)
They cannot vote for their own group.

Add up the marks and declare a winner.

Many people think our world was created by God, but however it was created, it's pretty amazing because there wasn't much around at the time to work with. Stop and think of all the different countries, different coloured people, trees, plants, mountains and seas, the sun, moon and stars. How were they created? I bet it took longer than 5 minutes. I wonder how many marks you would give it out of 5? Let's see.

Are there things or people that make you laugh in the world or make you think WOW!? **(Ask for suggestions.)** Vote now, marks out of 5 for imagination. **(Put mark in 4th column.)**

Now what about marks for use of materials. Are there lots of different materials? **(Take suggestions like wood, stone, water, skin, flesh, feathers.)** Are they used well? Vote now for use of materials **(Write up mark.)** Think about the whole world. What do you think of the finished product? Vote now. **(Write up mark.)**

(Add up marks and comment… depending on how the marks work out…) You obviously think someone made an excellent job of our world **or** looks like our world is an OK creation. And it goes on creating. **(Draw pictures.)** Volcanoes erupt and change shape, seeds fall and grow, every snowflake has a different pattern, animals and people are born. Let's give our groups and our world a round of applause. As we go around let's look out for new things our world is creating.

Variety is the spice of life

YOU WILL NEED

Scissors, paper, pencils/pens

Hands down!

Today we are celebrating! We are celebrating being different. Isn't it amazing that no two people are exactly the same. Even twins are different if you look close enough. Look at your own hands. Even though they are both yours, they are not the same. One might be bigger than the other, one might have a mark on it that the other one doesn't have. The lines and creases on each one will be different. What differences can you see? (*Give a little space for this and then pupils say what they have noticed.*) Isn't that interesting?

Does this mean that one hand is better than the other? Of course not! And do you know, your hands are very different from the hands of the person sitting next to you. Put your hand next to theirs. They are not the same are they? (*Again give space for this and responses.*) Isn't it good to be different! Life would be very boring if we were all the same. Give yourself a clap for being different!

Do you know the card game 'Snap!'? How do you play it? (*Pupils explain the rules.*) Well we're going to play snap with hands. First we need to draw round and cut out some hand shapes. (*Get at least four different sized people to come to the front for this and volunteers to help them.*)

Now I have all these different hands. Which one is the biggest/smallest? I'll shuffle them like a pack of cards, and the people who the hands belong to. (*Ask the people lined up to hold their hands out.*) Now let's see if we can play snap. I'll turn over a hand and we'll see if it matches the hand on the person. If it does, you can help me by shouting 'Snap!' (*Play the game.*)

Phew! That was exciting! We are lucky to be able to play that game. Just think if everybody was the same, we couldn't have played it could we? We wouldn't have had all that fun. It really is good to be different isn't it?

Prayers and Thinking

Sit quietly and look down at your own hands. Look at the back of your hands first. See how still and quiet you can keep them in your lap. Now turn them over and keep them still and quiet again. Your hands are amazing things and very special to you. Everybody has different hands. No one else has hands like yours. Take a moment to think about all the different and special things your hands can do.

Quote for the day

If we cannot now end our differences, at least we can help make the world safe for diversity.
John F Kennedy (1963) Address, American University, Washington DC 10th June

Faith links

Christian and Jewish
The diversity of animals taken into Noah's Ark
Genesis 6: 13–7: 5

Branching out

 Make some 3D 'Liquorice Alsort' mobiles from scrap materials, hang a positive phrase at the bottom of each one, e.g. Different but special.

 Make two photocopies of each pupil's hand. Muddle up the hands of the whole class and see if they can be correctly matched. You could also play snap with them.

 Compose a 'symphony of hands' from claps, taps, clicks, rubs, shakes, etc make a 'score' for this using photographs of the hand movements.

It takes 'allsorts'

PREPARATION NEEDED

Some 'Liquorice Allsorts'

A tray to tip them into

Some enlarged pictures
of the different 'alsorts'
to display round the
room (they do
photocopy quite well!)

WHAT TO DO

This assembly can be
told as a story narrated
by the assembly leader
or acted out by two
people.

If you can, finish the
assembly by sharing out
some 'alsorts' to taste.

Begin by holding up a
box of 'Liquorice Alsorts'
and asking if anyone
knows what they are. Tip
them out into a tray and
walk round with them so
that the audience can see
them.

What's so much fun about 'Liquorice Allsorts' is that there are lots of different sorts…in fact there are all sorts. Some are … pink…some are…blue… **(Get the audience to call out all the colours.)** Everyone has their own favourite. What's yours? Isn't it great that there are so many different ones? Yet they very nearly didn't turn out like this. Well so a story from Sheffield goes. That's where the sweets were first invented by a company called Bassetts. It was a long time ago, in 1899.

The salesman for Bassetts was called Charlie Thompson. And it was his job to take sweets round to different dealers to get them to buy them and then sell them on in their shops. Bassetts came up with a new line in liquorice sweets. It was Charlie's job to try and get someone interested in selling them. He took them to a big dealer in the town, carefully wrapped in boxes. But they didn't look quite like the 'alsorts' that we know and love. No…at that time the sweets were all kept separately. So all the round yellow ones were together in one box and all the square pink ones were together in another box…and so on. They were never mixed up. **(Invite children to sort them.)**

Charlie Thompson sat down at the table and laid out all the boxes of sweets in front of him. Very carefully, he opened each box one at a time and took out a sweet to show the dealer who sat opposite him. **"Ow abaht this yellerun?"** he said, holding it into the air for the dealer to see. **'Nay lad,'** said the dealer. **'Show me summat else!'** Charlie put the yellow sweet back in its box. Next he opened another box and this time held up a pink sweet. **'This'll tek tha fancy, I bet…'** But the dealer

gave it the thumbs down too. **'Nay lad, tha's hav ter do betterun that.'** Poor old Charlie went through each box in turn, holding up the different coloured and different shaped sweets and then putting them back into their boxes again. But each time the dealer said **'Nay lad, tha's westing thas time…and mine!'** In the end Charlie got so fed up he grabbed at all the sweets he had brought and went to stuff them back in his bag. But in his rush to get away, he dropped the boxes onto the table and all the sweets spilled out. And what was worse, they all got mixed up…the pinks with the blues, the blacks with the yellows, and the oranges with the browns and so on. **'Oh 'eck!'** cried Charlie, **'that's all I need!'** He began to scoop them into his hands. **"Ey up!"** shouted the dealer. **'Not suh fast lad…yuh might 'ave summat 'ere after all!'** The pair of them looked down at the table. The different coloured sweets looked so so bright and cheerful. **'Eee its just like a blummin' rainbow!'** said the dealer beaming at Charlie. **'I'll tek 'em.'** And from that moment on… Liquorice Allsorts were born…

These days 'Liquorice Allsorts' are sold all over the world. It's the mixed up colours and shapes that make them so popular. In some ways, you could say that people are a bit like 'alsorts'. We are all different aren't we? All different shapes and sizes. Long hair, short hair. Old and young. Different coloured skin and eyes. We have different likes and dislikes. Some people are good at one thing, some people another. Its being different that makes us so special. Just like Charlie's 'allsorts'. Wouldn't it be a shame, if we were all in our own separate little boxes instead of mixed up together making our own 'blummin' rainbow'?

Fair shares

The shrinking chapatti

YOU WILL NEED

Piece of paper, a pen and scissors

(Draw a chapatti shape on a piece of paper and cut it out. Check that everyone knows what one is.) There were once two friends who went for a walk. *(Ask for 2 volunteers.)* After a while they began to feel hungry. They came across a chapatti lying on a stone at the side of the road and began to argue about who should have it. 'Its mine,' said one, 'I saw it first.' 'No you didn't,' said the other, 'I did, so it's mine.' They started to push each other out of the way to get their hands on the food. Just then a stranger appeared *(Presenter plays this role.)* 'Stop it, both of you!' he called. 'The best thing to do is to share it. Here, I'll help you.' The stranger tore the chapatti in half and held up the two pieces. But one was bigger than the other. *(Do this with the paper.)* The two friends started to argue about who should have the biggest bit. 'I'm bigger than you so I should have the biggest bit.' 'No I should have it, I'm the smallest, so I need it most!' 'Oh no," sighed the stranger, 'I'd better try and make them even.' So he tore a piece off the biggest bit and ate it himself! *(Pretend to do this with the paper, crumpling it up and putting it in your pocket.)* But when he held up the pieces, one was still bigger than the other, so the stranger broke some more off the biggest bit and ate it. *(Repeat this routine a few times.)* Soon there were only two small pieces left. 'Oh dear!' sighed the stranger, 'now look what's happened, these are much too small to share out now,' so he ate the rest and walked off! The two friends stood open mouthed as they watched him walk away. Neither of them had had anything. 'If only we hadn't been so greedy!'

Prayers and Thinking

You will need either a pack of cards or a loaf of sliced bread. Share this out onto a table in four very uneven piles.

Think about the different countries in the world today. Is it fair that some have so much and others have so little? Wouldn't it be better if we all learned to share? **(Children help make the piles even.)** Help us to learn not to be greedy and to want more than we need. Help us to be fair and learn how to share with others.

Amen.

Quote for the day
There is enough in the world for everyone's need, but not enough for everyone's greed.
Frank Buchan (1947) *Remaking the World*

Faith links

Christian
The man who built bigger and better barns
Luke 12: 16-20

Sikh
Food sharing in the langar at the gurdwara

Branching out

Make shopping lists for a refugee or a homeless person.

Investigate the work of Oxfam, Christian Aid, or other local organisations that support those in need. Organise a fund-raising event.

Make some chapattis or cakes and invite some friends to a sharing party.

Shop 'til you drop!

Begin with the sound of coins spinning **(Three times.)** Then shake the rhythm of the first verse. **(No voices yet.)** The chorus should whisper the first few lines, gradually getting louder. Use different solo voices for the following verses, with chorus and percussion combining for the lines in bold. Shoppers should rush to and fro, grabbing boxes, carrier bags, etc. until they are piled high. Display picture images during verse four, as the shoppers stop and turn away. They resume shopping during the final verse, freezing just before the last line, which is spoken slowly by a soloist pushing through the shoppers to address the audience. Finish with the sound of coins spinning.

Shop 'til you drop.
Shop 'til you drop.
Spend! Spend! Spend!
Shop 'til you drop.
Shop 'til you drop.
Spend! Spend! Spend!

Grab it!
Nab it!
Pile it high!
Got to have it now.
Snatch it!
Clutch it!
Have to buy!
Doesn't matter how.

Want it!
Crave it!
Have to shop!
Buy up all the store.
Stash it!
Hoard it!
Just can't stop!
Must have more and more.

Never mind the hungry,
The homeless,
And the poor.
Close your eyes,
Switch off the news.
It really is a bore…so…

Shop 'til you drop.
Shop 'til you drop.
Spend! Spend! Spend!
Shop 'til you drop.
Shop 'til you drop…
…when will it end, end, end?

After the poem, ask the audience what they think about the shoppers. Why do they close their eyes and turn off the television? Practise the first and last verse with them and repeat the poem with the audience as the chorus for those sections.

A harvest for the world

The goodness lies in the soil

Prayers and Thinking

(Draw a large plate on a sheet of paper. Ask for suggestions of things poor people might need. Draw them on the plate.)
Think of those people and what you could do to help. You can ask God to give us kind hearts like *Jane* **or** (cabbage, eyes like potato and ears like wheat')

YOU WILL NEED

Flip chart/large sheet of paper with HARVEST printed at the top, marker pen

MIME SUGGESTIONS

Choose 2 volunteers to mime Joe and Jane. Tell pupils they have a part to play in this assembly. Divide assembly into 2 groups. Gp 1 chants 'It's not fair' and Gp 2 responds 'Learn to share'. Practise a few times

NB In the text... a word in [*CAPITALS*] = pupil to come out, find that word in the word HARVEST and write it on the sheet. [*] = point at groups to say their chant

(Point to HARVEST and ask assembly.) 'Can you find [**SHARE**]?' *(Write on flip chart.) (Continue with a story.)* Joe and Jane went to buy a field. Joe already had a big farm and was very rich. Jane was poor and needed to grow food for her family. The field was huge and had good soil. Jane could see it would cost too much and went away feeling very sad. Joe felt a bit sorry for Jane and said she could [**HAVE**] a very weedy piece of land. [*]

Jane worked really hard, but nothing grew. She looked at Joe's vegetables which grew bigger and bigger. Jane and her family grew more and more hungry. She went to Joe 'My family will [**STARVE**]' she said. 'Please may we have some of your food? I will repay you next year.' [*] "Grow your own" growled Joe, 'I've got plenty, I can [**REST**] and [**SAVE**] it all in my barn.' [*]

Jane was desperate and each night, when it was dark, went to Joe's dustbin to collect the food he threw away. [*] She put it into the pan of soup on her cooker. It didn't taste too bad and it was something to eat. One night, Jane looked out of her window. There was a fire, Joe's barn was alight. When Jane arrived, Joe's barn had burned down and all his food was gone. 'What am I going do?' wailed Joe. *(Ask pupils what he could do or what could happen.)* Let's see shall we?

Jane had a kind [**HEART**] and invited Joe's family to [**SHARE**] her soup. 'It's not much' said Jane 'but you are welcome to it.' 'I'm sorry,' said Joe 'next year let's work together in those fields, then we can share what we grow.' 'Is that fair?' What have we been telling them? [*]

Quote for the day
Justice begins with the recognition of the necessity of sharing.
Elias Canetti (1960)
Distribution and Increase Crowds and Power

Faith links

Christian
Feeding the 5000
Matthew 14:13

Jewish
Sukkot

Buddhist
Dana

Branching out

 Draw pictures of 'vegetable people'.

 Hot seat someone who has won the lottery. What will they spend it on? Will they give some away? To whom? Why?

 Find out what kind of food is eaten in other countries. Include Third World countries. Plan a day's menu for one rich, one poor country.

Food for thought

PREPARATION NEEDED

A basket containing a large potato, bunch of corn, cabbage

a pair of large (card) spectacles, a pair of large ears

a large red card heart

3 card masks: sad, angry, happy

sack of potatoes, loaf of bread, bag of sweets (optional) 2 mobile phones – someone primed to ring your number

WHAT TO DO

Have your basket conveniently placed among the harvest food

(Come in either with your hand to your ear as if listening or speaking into a mobile phone.) What! Well where are you? In a basket? I really can't believe I'm talking to a potato! Where's the basket? *(Cover the mouthpiece, address the pupils.)* Excuse me I'm just talking to a potato! Be with you in a minute. *(Go back to your phone. Audibly give yourself directions to where you have put the basket, as if someone is telling you.)*

(Pick up the basket and continue the conversation.) You're a bit squashed by the cabbage and the corn is tickling you? *(Rearrange the basket making sure the pupils see the potato.)* There, is that better? Now why did you ring me? You want me to tell the children something! *(Listen intently then put the phone down. Address the pupils.)* Potato said he's been using something, that you've all got, to learn about 'harvest'. Any ideas what potato has got that you've got? *(Take suggestions from the pupils. Give clues for EYES. Continue.)* Yes and he's been looking at the TV and reading the newspapers… he's seen that there are lots of people in our world who do not have anything to eat and are sick and starving. How does that make potato feel? *(A pupil comes out with a sad mask.)* Potato thinks they could do with some potatoes. *(Pupil comes to front with a sack of potatoes.)* Potato says we should look too, to see if there is anything we can do. *(Put large spectacles on a pupil and stand at the front.)*

(Phone rings. Answer it.) *(This time have a conversation with the wheat in the basket and relay it to the pupils. Follow the same pattern.*

Wheat is angry he has been using his EARS and has heard that there is enough food in our world for everyone but that some people are being greedy and have more than they need so there isn't any left for the poor. *Ask how that makes wheat feel – 1 pupil comes to the front with an angry mask.)* Wheat thinks they need some bread. *(Pupil comes with a loaf of bread. Put the card ears on a pupil and stand at the front.)* Wheat says we should listen to find out if there are any people in our town/village who do not have enough of the right food. Not even bread. *(Recap. Pointing to pupils with the specs and ears.)* What have potato and corn taught us so far? (To look out for and listen for people who do not have as much as we do.) *(All pupils join in the words underlined.)*

(Phone rings again. This time it's cabbage calling. Have an imaginary conversation following the same pattern as before.) 'Cabbage says that he has the most important thing of all. A HEART.' *(Give pupil the card heart to hold at the front.)* He can feel that there are generous, loving people here who care about people who are hungry and have brought food to share. *(Ask how that makes cabbage feel. Pupil with happy mask stands at the front. Two pupils come in sharing a bag of sweets.)*

(Recap, pointing to each of the card symbols.) So harvest gives us food for thought too. Potato wants us to look and learn about the poor countries. Wheat wants us to listen out for anyone we might be able to help. Cabbage wants us to share

Shalom

Sounds of silence

(Point to flip chart and ask pupils.) What
does peace mean? **(Point and ask.)** What
do you think this **!!*!** means?
Listen to this poem about noise. Think
what sort of noises it talks about?
**(Read poem, each verse begins and ends with
the lines in italics.)**

We're off to search for silent sounds
('Walk' on spot, hand above eyes.)
Come on then, let's go
(Indicate pupils to 'walk' quietly.)
I want to hear the sun rise
(Trace an arc with arm.)
Or the sound of falling snow
(Fingers make falling snow.)
Sshhh …listen. Can you hear them?
(Finger to lip – hand to ear – shake head.)

Come on – dive with me
('Dive' hands clasped above head.)
We might just hear the dolphins glide

(Fish movement with arm.)
Deep in the silent sea.
(Hold nose and 'duck'.)

Come on, creep with me
('Walk' on tip-toe, finger to lip.)
To hear the spider spin its web
(Hands up, wriggle fingers down.)
And clouds drift silently
(Arms out, floating movement.)

Come on – not a sound
(Finger to lip.)
Listen – there's a big fat worm
Wriggling underground
(Wriggle finger.)

Don't listen to the din
(Hands over ears.)
Of bang and crash – let's search for
peace
(Shake hands with neighbour.)
Come on now – don't give in

Let's read it again and you join in with
the actions. **(Reread.)** What were the
noises in the poem? **(As they name them
ask which column to write them in and why.)**
What noises in school stop it being a
quiet, peaceful place? **(Write ideas on flip
chart.)** When is school quiet and
peaceful? **(List on flip chart.)** How could
we make it more peaceful?

Prayers and Thinking

Sit quietly, hands on
knees. Breathe in slowly
to the count of 3 and
out to 3 (x3). Feel
peaceful and listen to
part of the prayer of St
Richard… 'Make me a
channel of your peace,
where there is hatred
let me bring love,
where there's despair,
hope.'

Quote for the day

Better a dry crust with
peace and quiet than a
house full of feasting
with strife
(Bible)

Faith links

Christian
Jesus stills the storm
Mark 4: 35

Buddist
Chittamasa

Branching out

 Find the word peace
in other languages,
e.g. shalom, pax, pace.
Make illuminated texts
of the words to put up
in school.

 Decide on some signs
pupils could use in
an argument to show
that they want to stop
and put things right
and a sign to agree.
Role play an
argument to practise.

 Sit in silence and
imagine all the
'quiet things' that
are going on
around you, e.g.
dust falling, insects
under the floor.

Sshhh!

PREPARATION NEEDED

Quiet music with someone to operate sound system

2 (easy) chairs

4 groups:
1. percussion/'rock' group
2. wearing football hats/scarves
3. arguing
4. with music player

Flip chart or OHP

NB. The aim of this assembly is to create the contrasts between peace and disturbance and feel the difference as you move from one to the other. *(Place finger to lip for the sound 'sshhh'.)*

As pupils assemble, a pupil is sitting in the easy chair, reading a book, listening to quiet music. At any noise, the leader says 'ssshhh' with a finger to their lips and points to the pupil in the chair.

When everyone has arrived, turn off the music and ask what the pupil is doing. *(Encourage words like quiet, soft, peaceful.)* Ask how you encouraged them to be quiet as they came in… What does 'sshhh' mean?

Tell them that you've had a hectic week *(give examples of being tired, cross, worried, etc.)*… you need some peace and quiet. So this morning in assembly, you are all going to be listening to quiet, peaceful music. Ask them to be considerate and not make any noise and if you do have to say 'sshhh' to anyone will they help you? *(Practise with them.)* Get 'comfy' in the other chair, finger to lip and 'sshhh' to the assembly and ask for the music to be put on again.

Immediately the percussion/rock group begins to 'play'. Leap up and encourage pupils to say 'sshhh' with you… Group stop. Ask someone to explain to the group what is happening in assembly this morning and why. Group sit down rather embarrassed.

Get comfy again, , 'sshhh', put on the music. This time the football fans come in chanting and waving their scarves and a fight breaks out…*(Repeat as for 'rock group'.)*

Repeat whole process with the group who start arguing and shouting and the group who start playing their music very loudly.

(In a whisper.) Tell the pupils you are going to give it one more go, put your finger to your lips and 'sshhh' After a few moments, stretch, get up and thank them. Tell them that has made you feel much better. *(If it doesn't happen tell them you will just have to try later in the day, but until then you might be a bit grumpy, and continue.)*

Ask when they might need peace and quiet (e.g. when they are tired, after an argument, when they feel angry) and what others can do to help…

Ask for suggestions of people in other parts of the world who might need some peace and quiet. *(List on flip chart.)* Ask why (noise, fear, killing, anger). Ask for ideas about how they could have peace.

What shall we say to all the people who make a noise and fight and argue or cause wars. *(All join in.)* Fingers to lips 'sshhh'.

All for one and one for all

All aboard the ark

YOU WILL NEED

Flip chart and marker. 5 pupils at the front to be the 'noise' leaders for: lion, monkey, cow, sheep, mouse. When their animal is mentioned they will jump up and lead the assembly in that noise.

WHAT TO DO

Draw ark outline, write/draw each animal as it is named. Practise each noise. Pupils join actions.

Story: Noah hit the last nail in the ark. 'Now,' said God 'I want you to get the animals inside.' So Noah's family went out calling (hand to mouth) the animals. 'Oh no,' moaned the cows, 'we don't want to be with those chattering monkeys.' 'And what makes you think we want to be with you?' jeered the monkeys, annoying other animals by jumping across their backs. 'Pack it in!' roared the lion, 'I can't think straight.' 'Don't shout,' squeaked the mice, 'you frighten us.' Everyone was pushing and shoving; they were making a terrible din. The sheep, were very hot and uncomfortable. They were terrified of the huge elephants, who took up so much room. The elephants were terrified of the mice who were trying to run up their trunks to get off the floor and everyone was getting very cross. 'Be quiet!' yelled Noah. Everyone stopped. It was so quiet you could hear a pin drop. It was so crowded, they could hardly breathe. The rain was falling outside and the ark began to float. (*All sway.*) It began to get a bit hot (*wipe brow*) and it got very smelly. (*Pinch nose.*) They all started arguing again; lion was feeling cold, (*shiver*) the monkeys were bored, (*fold arms*) the pigs were hungry (*rub tummy*) and the hippos were squashed. 'It's no good,' said Noah, 'If we are going to have a good trip, we must start thinking of each other.' 'You can have some of our wool,' said the sheep to the lions. 'I'll curl up to give hippo more room', said lion. 'And we can swing around to carry food to the pigs,' said the monkeys. 'What a grand idea,' said Noah, 'then you won't be bored.' Everyone tried to help. 'Well,' said Noah 'It won't be an easy ride but because you are all thinking how to help each other, I think we'll get along just fine.'

Prayers and Thinking

(*Draw an outline of the ark or a rocket.*) What can we do to make people happier in school? (*Write in the suggestions. Read through the suggestions.*) Look at the **rocket/ark.** Think of one thing you could do, or pray 'Help us Lord, to work and play so everyone is happy.'

Quote for the day

Self-preservation has a tendency to lead to poverty
Jim Rohn (2001) *Excerpts from The Treasury of Quotes*

Faith links

Christian
The Early Church
Acts 4, Exodus 16: 32–37

Muslim
The Hajj or Umra

Branching out

 Put an outline of the ark on the wall. When a pupil puts someone else first in class, write it in the ark.

 In groups play picture consequences to design a character. Two or three groups work together to make up a play for their characters.

 Plan a class trip/activity, finding suitable jobs for everyone, e.g. handing out lunches, pouring drinks, looking after anyone who feels unwell, being a friend, etc.

Light the blue touch paper

PREPARATION NEEDED

Large imitation
fireworks – Rocket,
Airbomb, Silver Rain,
each with description
label

packet of sparklers

table laid out as a shop
counter with fireworks
behind in a box

Sam and his dad, Tim
and his grown up
brother, Susie and her
gran, Jane,
Mr Jones the shopkeeper

3 chairs

WHAT TO DO

Practise firework noises
to be made when each
firework is mentioned.
Rocket = 'Whoosh'
Airbomb = 'Boom'
Silver Rain = 'Weeeee'
(Characters enter as they
are *named.)

Begin the story

*Mr Jones ran the local shop. He sold comics, cleaners, tissues and all the things a local shop sells. Every November he sold other things too… **(Ask what that might be.)** Mr Jones holds up box. *Sam had been saving his pocket money to buy some fireworks. He was looking round with his dad when suddenly he saw the giant fireworks. 'What are they?' he asked. 'They cost a lot' said Mr Jones **(He reads the descriptions.)** 'Cor the Airbomb, that's the one for me. I make more noise than anyone round here. I'll spend all my money on the Airbomb. Those small ones are rubbish!' **(Sam walks off very pleased making loud booming noises.)**

Later *Tim comes into the shop with his grown up brother. 'I've just earned some money cleaning dad's car. What fireworks have you got Mr Jones?' **(Mr Jones shows him the sparklers.)** 'Or I have…' **(Shows him the other two large fireworks and reads the descriptions.)** 'Wow, I'll have the Rocket Racer, I can go faster than anyone on my skateboard. The Rocket Racer's for me for me, it's worth all my money and the sparklers are silly.' **(Walks away delighted making the rocket noise.)**

Later that day *Susie ran into the shop with her gran 'Oh Mr Jones, my gran has given me some money for fireworks, have you any left?' **(Mr Jones shows her the packet of sparklers.)** 'I don't want those' she yelled, 'what about that one?' and she pointed to the Silver Rain. 'It's expensive,' said Mr Jones, 'but it is very pretty.' 'Then that's the one for me, I'm the prettiest girl in my school so Silver Rain must have been made for me.' said Susie.

(She walks away admiring her firework and tidying her hair.) It began to grow dark, *Susie kept looking at her Silver Rain, she was looking forward to seeing all the silver stars. But she really wanted Sam and Tim to enjoy it too.

*Sam couldn't wait to let off his Airbomb, but it would be much more fun to let other people share it and he had bought the only one 'Oh dear,' thought *Tim 'what's the use of paying all that money just for me to see a Rocket. It could be the grand finale of a firework party, then everyone will see it.'

They all sat down to think **(all sit)**. 'I know,' said Sam. 'I know,' said Tim. 'I know,' said Susie, 'I'll see if I can share my firework with someone else, then we'll have a big display. Soon a large crowd had gathered in the field next to Sam's house. The grown ups collected all the fireworks and arranged to set them off. What a sight! Catherine wheels, jumping jacks, Sam's Airbomb made such a deafening explosion everyone screamed and Susie's Silver Rain poured out so many silver stars she thought it would never stop. Tim's Rocket shot up to the moon to finish the show. Just as they were all feeling a bit sad Jane came over 'Would you like to share my sparklers? I couldn't afford big fireworks but it would be fun to light them together.' It was the perfect end to a brilliant night.

(Ask how sharing and working together could make things better for our world.)

(Alternative suggestion: each buy favourite CD and end up with a disco or prepare a national dish and have a party.)

Signs for The thirsty crow
(Patience, p 61)

HOT	Wipe brow.
SUN	Draw circle in air with finger, compress fingers on thumb then open wide.
WATER	Palm down, make wavy movement at side of body.
NONE LEFT	Hold hands palm up and shake head.
BIRD	Compress fingers on thumb, point outwards at side of mouth and open and close for beak.
FLY	Hands flat, hook thumbs, fly hands up.
RIVER	Hold hands apart, palms facing moving forward making a winding shape.
DRINK	Mime drinking from a glass.
TIRED/REST	Palms together, rest cheek on hands as if on pillow.
THIRSTY	Pluck throat with index finger and thumb.
CROW	Bird, + with other hand make 'c' with thumb and finger.
DROP	Hold compressed fingers high in air and then open them.
BUCKET	Hands together, palms upwards with little fingers touching, draw rising hands apart to shape side of bucket, then right hand mimes lifting handle.
IN/INSIDE	Hold left hand as horizontal 'c' shape, compress fingers of right hand and put inside 'c'.
LITTLE	Hold right first finger short distance from right thumb.
STONE	Close left fingers on palm, draw small circle on back of right hand.

References

Booth T, Ainscow M, Black-Hawkins K, Vaughn M, Shaw L (2000) *Index for Inclusion: Developing Learning and Participation in Schools'*. Bristol: Centre for Studies on Inclusive Education.

Corbett J (2002) Inclusion *Special Children*, April.

Goleman D (1996) *Emotional Intelligence*. London: Bloomsbury.

Howlin P, Baron-Cohen S, Hadwin J (1999) *Teaching Children with Autism to Mind Read*. Chichester: Wiley.

Shaw S, Hawes T (1998) *Effective Teaching and Learning in the Primary Classroom'*. Leicester: The SERVICES Ltd.

Index